Real Estate

Dad's Way

Updated from

Buy a Boarded-up House with Contents

Jeff Cooper

Jeff's book is packed with many interesting facts, figures, and insights into the local real estate market. As a real estate appraiser and broker, he discusses many rules of thumb on evaluating real estate opportunities. He shares many local, personal real estate experiences in which he and his father participated in the Palatka area. I enjoyed his comments on his personal experience with many real estate leaders in our area.

William A. ("Bill") Watson, Jr., President, Watson Realty Corp., REALTORS

***

This book should be a best seller for the small town market. For those who are getting in the real estate business, it is very practical, down to earth, and tells how it really happens in the smaller market. I re-read parts of it all the time, and have for several years.

Lloyd Adams

***

I have enjoyed it immensely and had many laughs from it also, certainly, everyone interested in real estate—agent or not—should make this book a "must read"! Our two sons want it next.

William H. Houston, M.D.

My favorite bit of advice from Cooper: "People can't see what you eat, only what you wear. Eat hash and buy good clothes."

Fred Seely, Editorial Director,

Realty/Builder Connection

Dear Reader:

Arthur E. Cooper's early success buying property impressed me. His first and stunning success came when I was 6 years old.

He made $4,000 on his first deal in 1949! Why didn't he stay in Fox Chapel and do it again? Why didn't he stay in my birthplace, Las Vegas? Rates of return are figured on lump sum cash basis, with no effect given for terms, expenses, tax considerations and management.

I am Jeff Cooper, Art's only child. My Realtor career started in Jacksonville and Palatka in 1968. Dad was my father, friend and business partner.   A great deal of emotion goes into buying a home. There is a feeling that "If I don't get this house, I will die." This is a seller's delight. Your job as real estate investor is to find the "don't-wanter." Great real estate men often go broke because they buy or borrow too much. Dad was never put off by an ugly or run-down building. "Well bought is half sold".

If you've ever worked with your parents, this book's for you.

Real estate is an excellent savings tool. Buyers can be elusive.

An enthusiastic person often hasn't had time to know the downside. But you can be too well informed. Tone your conversations as if you were being recorded.

A home is a shelter first and an investment second. Most progress occurs through caring. Some of the deals in this book are historic, but the principles remain valid. Real Estate is still a good investment.

A big company can pay an obscenely high price for your property and it has no effect on their balance sheet.

One good Realtor on your side for life can make you a fortune. Since I live in Florida, the book has a Florida slant. Real estate has certain expenses and uncertain income.

Thanks to Lee Meadows, John Meadows, John Rogers, Earl Miller, Rod Porter, Parker Reynolds, Jim Pace, Ben Strode, Robert W. Coffman, Mike Malaghan, Jonathan Cooper and Ted Hornoi-Centerwall.

Thanks to my wife, Martha, family and clients. It is my clients who have educated me.

The difference between the "haves" and the "have-nots" is whether you own real estate. It divides the world into "mouths" and "wallets".

Don't act on the advice of this book without asking knowledgeable professionals. Laws and conditions change and I could be wrong.

Dedicated to

Arthur Edwin Cooper

1901-1998

Table of Contents

Have Good Parents

Dad, Arthur E. Cooper, was born in 1901. He was one of eight children. Granddad gave up coal mining in Kentucky and moved the family to South Dakota. There he got a homestead which was 160 acres of free land given by the government, provided you lived on it and worked it. They built a sod house, and shot or grew their food. They raised cattle, an occupation that Granddad had the rest of his life and two of Dad's brothers did, too.

There were seven boys and one girl. Dad bonded with Conrad, who was two years younger. For Christmas they each got an orange or an apple. One banner year they got both! They worked hard and didn't realize they were poor. When a neighbor dropped in, you fed him, whether you had enough or not. The children became a team with lifelong ties. Later when Dad earned a normal wage, he thought he was rich.

Mother was from South Dakota and married my father in 1938. Their marriage lasted for life. Mother had one year of college but read more than Dad. She was a secretary but didn't work after I was born in 1943.

Dad became a real estate broker in Palatka, Florida in 1957 when I was 14. One day I was watching the office for him and kept some customers from leaving until he got back. He sold them a $10,000 house and earned a $600 commission. I was impressed.

Our store front real estate office welcomed all. Friends would sit and talk and the needy would pick up trash to earn $2. Dad's filing system was simple: new stuff in front, important stuff on the desk top and the really important stuff in his shirt pocket.

Dad bought a dozen real estate parcels and never left Putnam County. He never paid over $25,000 for anything and never defaulted on a debt.

I painted houses and cleared land. They told me getting good grades was my main job. I got a degree in real estate from the University of Florida and four years later, Dad and I were working together.

My parents liked good clothes, bought nearly new cars and kept them a long time. They went to church, didn't drink and made frugality a job. Mother hated debt and was against everything, so Dad battled for each mortgage.

Dad said: "Ethics is like a sheet of paper. Wad it up and then try to straighten it out." He'd say: "One good investment is worth a lifetime of toil."

As Dad and Mother aged they bought CDs, certificates of deposit. I think Dad thought of them as war bonds. You could borrow on a CD paying 2% above what you were getting. In 1981 interest rates skyrocketed and Dad borrowed on all his CDs, paying the higher interest and received even more interest. The bank finally changed the rules prohibiting this.

He only bought one stock: U.S. Steel because his brother Conrad had now worked his way up to Vice President of the steel company. The stock lost money.

Mother got cancer in 1959 and later emphysema. Despite these maladies, she lived to be 80. Mother was well read and had lots of opinions. Dad took good care of her throughout her difficult times. I never worried about them having affairs or getting a divorce.

Buy an Un-built House in a Good Neighborhood

We lived in hotels or furnished apartments. Everything we owned could fit in the black 1948 Olds four-door 88.

In 1949, Dad got a job with a moving company in Pittsburgh. He was a manager but clashed with the owner. Still, the money was good and we bought a house from plans in Fox Chapel, a nice rolling wooded subdivision.

I was six years old in 1949. We visited the site often and I wandered through the stud walls. I loved the smell of fresh cut lumber.

The deep lot seemed huge and sloped down to a creek in back. I thought of damming the creek. One day a boulder dislodged and rolled toward me. They yelled and I side-stepped a near disaster.

I watched the house form into two stories, and the brick being applied. One of the workmen had a mini motorcycle. I inspected it carefully and knew I could ride even though I'd never been on a bicycle.

Relations with Dad's boss worsened and he resigned. He sold the Fox Chapel house before it was completed. His contract price was $20,000 and the sale price was $24,000. This was the beginning of modern real estate inflation.

What to do now? Not to worry. He saw an ad in the *Wall Street Journal* "Sale Florida fish camp cheap." I was excited about living on the river in Florida but was to miss Fox Chapel. The camp only had a cottage and I slept on a couch bed.

My parents were not to own a real house for another 14 years. Mother hated Florida and missed our grand home. So near but so far, she thought.

The fish camp was pounding hard work. The easy money was to be made by staying in Fox Chapel and buying more houses. Opportunity had clobbered my father and still he didn't see it.

Suppose the house was worth $700,000 by 2010. That's a return of 5.8% per annum due to the 60 year holding period. One good buy is all you need.

Buy a Florida Fish Camp

I was fortunate to fly at age 7. We took off from the Pittsburgh airport in 1950. Sun streamed in the windows of the four-engine plane. This ride was better than anything Disney came up with years later. I panicked when the plane banked but enjoyed the rest of the flight.

When we landed in Jacksonville, Florida, it was hot. I had only one reference to temperature. When we lived in Ohio, one day it was hot and when I asked Mother how hot, she said 80°. Riding in the car through the Putnam County countryside it was 95 humid degrees. My shirt clung like wet tissue. When the car stopped, I heard a strange noise; bugs, millions of them.

Magnolia Bluff fish camp was eight acres on the St. Johns River. It was 15 miles south of Palatka and 75 miles south of Jacksonville, The land sloped and our access road was a dirt rut. The elevation change must have been 50 ft. from the hard road to our land.

There were eight cabins huddled in the center near the river. The riverbank was about 10 feet. An uncovered dock leaned and tilted. There was a handy-man trailer and old wooden barn of 1,000 square feet.

I spotted the Spanish moss which hung from every tree and looked like an old man's beard. Mother didn't like it either. I thought, how to get rid of it: there are so many trees. Within two weeks I was used to this now all but extinct air plant. At night the moon gave everything a haunted look.

Dad's hobby was fishing. The seller took him out and he caught two bass on one hook. Dad was hooked, too, and paid the full asking price of $25,000. The seller, Monroe, was jubilant.

Twelve boats were mostly rotten. One by one we pulled them up on the bank, filled them with dirt and made them into worm farms; then bought new boats. Paying as we went, Dad built a cover for the dock. During a Florida summer day it can rain a dozen times and the boats have to be free of water for renting.

We owned six kickers (outboard motors) ranging from five to ten horsepower and there was a block minnow tank. We had everything but food and liquor. Customers brought their own booze and we had to rescue a few drunks from the river.

The well water was undrinkable. We bought water in ten gallon bottles from a delivery truck. We dug five wells but none were suitable for drinking. For $10 an old black man held out his divining rod (forked stick) and walked the camp until a vibration happened. We dug there and found pure water.

We had a 36 inch cycle mower which pulled itself, shook and roared. Dad mowed as much of the square eight acres as he could. One day, wind felled a tree across our rut road and, against Dad's advice, I axed it, almost losing a toe.

I painted cabins and got up at 4 a.m. to dig worms. Dad carried kickers for customers and we cleaned some of their fish. Mother cleaned cabins, but not happily. Dad made friends with the Palatka paper sports writer, Fred P. Green. I loved that name and gave him a brother, I Pee Daily. Many articles extolled the virtues of fishing at Magnolia Bluff.

Hunter, our part time handyman, lived in the trailer. He wore no shirt and carried a Bowie knife. He'd swig out of his hip pocket pint and fling the knife at a tree, sticking it with deadly accuracy. He took offense at a customer's dog and nicked his leg. Hunter had to go.

Then our work increased and we could not leave. We became friends with some repeat customers and they would watch the camp for us, but not for long. When the plumbing would burst on a weekend, we had no access to the store until Monday.

Dad built the business up. He had fishing contests and one of our customers was a professional photographer. Pictures of fish and fishermen were everywhere. Customers gathered in our cabin to watch the only black and white TV on the premises. The drink machine had Cokes in glass bottles for 5 cents.

I used the barn to make things, like the rocket I launched. It spewed upward and caught in a tree. Damn, I thought, two days to make that rocket and it's gone. Anger turned to fear as the moss ignited. No fire truck could get down our rut road, even if one was nearby. The fire burned itself out but to this day I always notice the proximity of fire hydrants.

Years later when I cleaned out the files, I realized how badly Dad wanted to sell the camp. He was 56 years old and had gained a lot of weight cooking for himself. Mother and I lived in an apartment in Palatka during the week for my school and her sanity.

He sold the camp in 1956 for $37,000. That buyer sold it for $55,000. By 1991 the land was worth $250,000. That represented 6.6% per annum compound growth.

In other words, if you put our price of $25,000 in the bank drawing 6.6% interest, in 35 years you'd have $250,000. Land doesn't spend like cash and can bankroll a nice retirement.

We should have kept one of the eight acres. The camp parcel was about 600 ft. on a side. One acre at either end would be 73 ft. by 600 ft. The cabins were in the center of the land. Today, the one acre would be worth $200,000. The value or our sale price should not have been affected. Our cost basis for one acre was $3,125 ($25,000 / 8). From 1950 to 2010 is 60 years which is 7.2%/annum. We were not real estate wise. Dad's people skills were to come in handy on his next job; real estate broker.

By 1982, the camp had become a subdivision known as Magnolia Bluff Estates.

Buy an Ocean Condo

Dad's younger brother was Richard Conrad Cooper, Uncle Conrad. He was two years younger than Dad and they paired growing up on the cattle ranch in South Dakota. They both graduated from the University of Minnesota. Dad had a degree in forestry and Conrad was a civil engineer.

Conrad worked for Wheeling Steel and later U.S. Steel. By World War II Conrad has a reputation for hard bargaining. After the war he became chief negotiator for the industry against big labor. Big steel was the national bellwether and holding down inflation was the business of government. Conrad met presidents Eisenhower, Kennedy and Johnson.

Conrad and his wife, Irene, lived in Sewickley, near Pittsburgh. They wintered in Del Ray Beach (north of Miami, Florida). They'd rent an oceanfront suite for two weeks and we'd drive from Palatka to visit.

They rented the same unit from 1950 until 1955 when they bought a two bedroom condominium in the Carlton House. It was on the third floor and had a view of the Atlantic Ocean and the

Intra-coastal Waterway. The price was $35,000. The condos were called clubs to keep out Jews.

Those were great times. Irene got tanked on martinis while Conrad quietly slipped into oblivion on scotch. He smoked cigars, too! I watched this as a boy and young man. The example was not missed.

Irene had mink jackets and platinum hair. She furnished the unit lavishly, including $50 pillows. Mother fumed. Not only was mother a teetotaler but she looked on excessive spending as a sin.

Dad adored Conrad and I knew the best way to be loved was to be like him. We'd eat in some expensive restaurant that served alcohol. Conrad always rented a new car, too. One year he handed me the keys to a Chevrolet Impala convertible. I was trusted to drive all five of us because at 17, I didn't drink much.

Conrad died in 1981 at age 79. Irene followed three months later. Their attorney had asked me to sell the unit. I checked with local Realtors and valued it at $165,000.

The Goldbum's already lived in Carlton House but in a one bedroom. They wanted a two bedroom and called me. My wife, Martha, and I drove down.

Mr. and Mrs. Goldbum met us at the unit and gasped at the furnishings. We settled on a price of $145,000. I said, "We are spending the night and taking some things with us in the morning. Whatever is left, you can have."

We bedded down with the windows open. The breeze whipped the curtains and moaned. I had not spent the night in Del Rey since my uncle and aunt had died. It was eerie. I wandered around, looking at their glorious possessions, which now was just "stuff."

Sunrise on the ocean is beautiful. The Goldbums were there early, shadowing us like basketball players. We stuffed the Mustang with a TV, golf clubs, silver, mirrors, gadgets and mementos. I wished we had brought the Olds. Goldbum paid cash but the title company didn't want to take Conrad's power of attorney. I got $1,000 commission.

Conrad's estate was cash poor, but Goldbum didn't know this. Neither was the unit ever exposed on the open market. I was motivated, too. I wanted this trip to be the last trip. The seller, Mellon Bank trust department, required no appraisal.

The selling price of $145,000 represents a growth of 5.3% per annum on the $35,000 purchase price. This low rate is due to the long holding period of 27 years.

Buy a Burned Estate and Fix It Up

Regardless of value, an estate is any property where the owners have died.

Conrad and Irene bought an estate in 1949. It was part of the Woodland Tract in the posh Pittsburgh suburb of Sewickley.

What they bought was the land, seven acres located near a small mountain top. Tall trees abounded and you could see the Ohio River in the distance. Noise of a big city filtered up and I always enjoyed the cool climate compared to Florida.

The original house had burned. My aunt and uncle lived in the servants' quarters above the garage. Gradually they built and added to their home, which was three stories in front and one story in back due to the slope of the land. The address was classy; #2 Woodland Road.

A narrow private road wound up the hill. One winter we got stuck in the snow. I remember the moon shining on huge snow-covered evergreen trees. A yard man kept the grounds and trees were recessed in giant cups. Irene built a greenhouse.

Once I got locked in a bathroom for what seemed like hours. No one could hear me banging away in that huge place. Another time, I got lost walking down the hill. Finally a neighbor returned me, but the police had already been called.

Their house epitomized wealth and power. One Christmas up there, I got a bicycle and an electric train, an amazing difference from Dad's orange and apple. Equally amazing was the garage door opener and remote control TV. My parents never had any covering over their cars.

By 1982 Conrad and Irene were dead. They had no children and the Mellon Bank managed their property. After the house was stripped of its contents, you could see all the dirt and cigarette butts. The appraisal was $350,000.

The floor plan was unique and over 5,000 sq. ft. Sewickley passed an ordinance stating that Conrad could not subdivide his seven acres due to the narrow access road. The house didn't sell even after the bank spent $25,000 fixing it up.

After over a year, an offer was accepted for $260,000 but it was contingent upon the buyer getting a bank loan, which he was not able to do. Finally, after two years on the market, the property sold for $240,000, 31% off its appraised value.

Estate buying can be a powerful money builder. Disinterested banks or churches often sell property for a fraction of its value. It's found money to heirs who often don't care about the value, either. Some heirs are poor or have pre-spent through borrowing and will take anything. Most heirs are emotionally distraught and many never want to see the place again. They will deep discount to sell fast. Wealth does not come with an owner's manual.

Buy on the Edge of Town near Something Important

After Dad sold the fish camp, he became a real estate broker. Back in 1957 you just went to Orlando and took the broker's test. If you passed it, you were a broker.

He rented an upstairs office in downtown Palatka. Those stairs were dark and steep. One day I surprised a man sleeping up there.

Dad bought 10 acres near a proposed junior college on the edge of Palatka. Access was by rut road. It had pine trees and a paint-less shack full of bottles.

Dad gave me permission to shoot up the shack. I had a 22 semi-automatic rifle. I approached the shack with my rifle at waist level. It fired every time the trigger was pulled and I splattered wood and glass everywhere, just like Elliot Ness.

Gradually the college was built and the road was extended nearer our land. Finally, the college was finished. It was one of the first in Florida.

Dad paid $8,500 for the land and a year later sold it for $16,000 – a return of 65%. A survey was ordered and we discovered the bullet riddled shack was not on our land.

In 1960 Dad bought 10 acres near a new hospital. It had a small block house which Dad made into his office. I painted the building and lay out back sunbathing. Tanning was not for me.

I watched the office for him, but knew this was a lousy office site with almost no traffic. What I didn't know was that Dad had a secret source of income.

He paid $9,000 for this plot and a year later sold it for $14,500 – a return of 42%. Sleepy Palatka had 9,000 people back then. I wondered what Dad could have done had we stayed in my birth town, Las Vegas.

Tracts on the edge of town can be good investments because major improvements can't go closer in due to small ownerships. Good locations are not secret, just read the newspaper. Good buys can be had for years after a project is announced.

Dad was right to sell at a profit. The hospital eventually became a nursing home and the junior college enrollment fell from its opening, 3,500 down to 1,200 as many other colleges were built in Florida. Other improvements built in this area included a high school, a trailer park, and a low income apartment complex.

It's easy to see how I figured you can't go wrong buying real estate.

The key to high returns in real estate is short ownership times.

Trade a Car for a Lot

When I was a freshman at the University of Florida, I bought my first car. I paid $168 for a 1949 black Pontiac convertible, a straight "8" that drove like a truck. It had red interior and the power top failed. I had to wrestle it up and down by hand, and when I stood up in the back, I crunched through the floor.

Beginning the sophomore year, I was in trouble. The pre-engineer curriculum was killing me. I dropped out and re-entered as a business major in real estate. Dad was not excited, but I was not to know why for many years.

I found a '55 Chevy two-door hardtop with white sidewall tires and glass pack mufflers. It had a Georgia tag and *Playboy* magazines in the trunk (a good omen).

I cashed in all my savings bonds and paid the full asking price of $595 plus tax. The dealer, Coleman, chomped on his cigar and beamed.

The glass packs roared beautifully but the engine died all the time. Coleman said the engine was tight, as it had just been rebuilt. I asked "Why was it rebuilt?"

He said, "Son, any engine with 99,000 miles on it needs to be rebuilt."

"Oh," I said, I hadn't noticed the mileage.

The tires popped like bubblegum. One night the wiring caught fire and the lights flickered and went out. The engine began knocking and rattling. I checked on the place that rebuilt the engine and found a vacant building.

I was beaten. I drove the smoking car to Dad's real estate lot, put a "for sale" sign on it and bought a bicycle.

The car still looked great and many people wanted it, but money was short. Some country folks looked and Dad got to talking. Although they had no money, they did have a vacant lot. Dad traded it for the car and one year later he sold the lot for $700.

I want back to the car lot (scene of the crime) and waited for Coleman. I thanked him for selling me the Chevy, as we made a $100 profit. His cigar fell in his lap.

Today, the car would be worth $50,000.

Buy a Boarded-up House with Contents

Dad and mother only lived in one house that they owned. The fish camp had a cottage and we didn't live in it full time, nor did we own the entire camp.

They found Emmett Street in 1963. It was one block off the St. Johns River in old Palatka. I was at the University of Florida and came home on break to look.

It was a narrow, tall, painted red Victorian house sitting high on brick piers with a high pitched metal roof. The lot was 50 ft. x 150 ft. A wrap-around one story front porch set off the two story place.

Stained glass windows were 8 ft. high. Immediately upon entering there was a red staircase. New carpet was deep shag. To the left was a five-sided living room with dark green Gothic wallpaper.

Gas lamps hung from the ceiling, but were wired for electricity. The den or dining room had burled stained wood wainscoting. The kitchen was remodeled with ponderosa pine cabinets, brick accents and had the only air conditioning unit.

There were three fireplaces outfitted with gas logs. The house had only 1,700 sq. ft. It was built about 1878. There were two bedrooms with an interconnecting bath upstairs. The leg tub and vanity had gold leaf faucets and lewd wallpaper.

I was pleasantly surprised that my parents wanted this gaudy house. We had always lived in modest apartments.

The seller was a hairdresser named Richard. Dad paid him $10,000 over five years at 4% interest. Dad thought 30 year mortgages were a fool's journey.

Right after we moved in, Dad had to replace a rotten sill; a large wooden timber under the house. He didn't know to get a termite inspection before closing.

Eventually they put a bathroom in the large downstairs closet. The attic was huge and unobstructed by trusses but there was no insulation or floor. Despite the bedrooms reaching oven-like heat levels, they never air-conditioned the upstairs.

The house sold in 1994 for $45,000 – a return of 4.9% per annum over the 31-year holding period.

Richard bought the house in 1960. It was built as a spite house and sat real close to the neighbor and further out in front. An original owner, G. Loper Bailey's ghost was said to still be there.

In 1925 the last owner died. There being no more heirs, the will called for a church to inherit. The church boarded it up and let it sit. It sat vacant for 35 years. I used to walk past it as a boy and imagine Alfred Hitchcock inside, knifing someone in a shower. I would have died had I known I'd be living in the paint-less edifice.

Richard offered the church $3,500 and they accepted without hesitation. The house was not appraised or exposed for sale in the open market.

He opened the house and found it was full of contents... clothes, dishes, silver, furniture – all period 1880s. In the attic were trunks full of Confederate money in original bank wrappers.

Richard sold most of the contents and recouped his entire investment. He moved in and spent the next two years refinishing it. Dad and mother got a few of the antiques and I now have them.

After selling to my parents, Richard opened an antique store in Orange Park south of Jacksonville.

Sell in One Day

In 1959, Dad bought a lot in South Florida for $990 with $10 down and payments of $10 a month. It was in Port St. Lucie by General Development Corp. Dad felt sorry for the down at the heels salesman.

Dad knew how to fire my imagination. He gave the lot to me. I drove down to see it. The General Development office was easy to find, but the lot was not. Under the terms of the contract for deed, they had 10 years to build the road to it. That's how long it took to pay it off at $10 a month.

Ten years later I went back. This time the road was paved and I found the lot and installed the "for sale" sign. There were only a few houses built and grass was growing through the road. Many other sale signs were up.

By 1975 I was suffering in the recession resulting from the imported oil embargo. I drove to nearby Fort Pierce, got a motel room and the next day presented myself at the largest real estate office in town.

Salesman Sam greeted me warmly, but cooled when he found out all I had to sell was a Port St. Lucie lot. He had thousands of these lots for sale. I said, "I'm from Jacksonville and I want to sell this lot today." He thumbed through his book. All the lots were priced at about $3,000. I said, "Name your price." He looked at my contract and went to a map on the wall.

He said $2,000 and I said, "Sold!"

I went back a month later for the closing. Sam said, "Let's drive out to the lot and inspect the fill." Fill, I thought, what fill? Under the terms of the contact for deed, General Development also had 20 years to fill any lots needing fill, provided you notified them in advance of your need. When we got to the lot, there was a gaping hole in the lot next to mine but mine had been topped off with fresh dirt. Sam said okay! Whew, I thought, that was close.

We doubled our money in 16 years, which was 4.3% per annum, minus trips and motel. Dad was happy. He was afraid I'd give it away since my cost basis was nothing.

General Development's creative methods were criticized and the recession of 1990 pushed them into bankruptcy. There was a scandal over the inflated appraisals and deceptive sales practices.

You should not buy sight unseen, as Dad did. He figured it was so cheap he couldn't lose. General Development and its more unscrupulous cousins have given Florida a bad name for land investments.

Study Real Estate

There were four professors at the University of Florida Real Estate department in 1963.

Dr. Ring, head of the department, was author of the appraisal textbook. He told dirty jokes and laughed louder than any of us. Dr. Curtis also wrote a book. I liked him but he mumbled and was hard to understand. Dr. Sheinkel was a detail man and boring. A woman professor whose field was architecture rounded out the group.

I sat for the Florida real estate license exam at age 21. I was on my second college term, so breezed over the handbook. After failing the exam, I memorized the handbook and passed easily the second time.

Dr. Ring was a pedantic man and a bully. He beat the material into us and had the only courses of substance that I can remember. Being a Ring graduate give us prestige in the job market.

I remember the excitement of doing my first appraisal as a student, for Fred Arnold, a Gainesville Realtor whose office was near the campus. I pawed through his files for the comparable data. Later I found out he was one of Dad's clients and his wife owned many low grade rentals in Palatka.

I enjoyed the downtown study I did for Dr. Curtis. I also did a talk on interlocking business relationships in small towns. It was called, "The banker is the brother-in-law of the builder."

I had a part-time job with a home builder named Kirkpatrick. His son, George, was a few years older than I. I sat in model homes each weekend and was paid $1 an hour. I would have gotten a commission, but never made a sale. Homes were looked at over the weekend, but bought during the week.

A black couple dropped by the model. George, in shirt and tie, told them he was just the maintenance man; then he went and hid.

Having access to these homes and business was very useful when I did the demonstration appraisal report for Dr. Ring.

George had a friend, Bert Rogers, who ran the largest private license prep school at the time. He asked me to pass out brochures in class. When I did this, Dr. Ring exploded. I had insulted his educative powers. I felt then that college didn't do enough to prepare one for real life.

On weekend, I'd help Dad with his work and appraisals. I was able to tell the class about real deals and took real knowledge home to Dad.

Another great part-time job was field man for Howze & Associates. They were re-appraising Putnam County for real estate tax purposes. During the summer I worked in Palatka. I measured buildings and filled out field feature cards. This data was then keypunched into a huge IBM computer in Tampa, very advanced for 1963.

I counted fireplaces. The system gave them $500 each and one old house had seven, which made fireplaces half the property's value. Vacant upper floors of downtown buildings were given 60% of first floor value, even though they had produced no income for years.

Despite these glitches, I was impressed enough to work for Howze & Associates after graduation.

Work in Taxation

I started work in Pensacola, Florida in 1966 as a land appraiser. We had a big room at the courthouse and there were about 10 employees.

Florida passed a law mandating assessments to be at 100% of fair market value. This set off a spate of re-appraisals and other states followed suit.

Escambia County supplied us with aerial maps and ownership maps with comparable sales written on them. I rode by the land to be appraised and then wrote values on the ownership maps.

It was tricky. Other appraisers working adjacent maps might be twice as high as me or half my values. It's more important to be consistent than accurate.

My friend Parker had a VW Bus. He pulled the seats and installed a table. We'd take maps into the field and attempt to code values outside, but I couldn't concentrate. All the dust from the dirt roads fouled the air-cooled engine and the bus burned up.

I lived in Shea's Tiki house on Pensacola Beach, a motel on pilings with cars parked underneath. Bill Ferris got me into the Army Reserve and I went to meetings for two years in Pensacola before switching to Palatka. I was engaged to Linda at the time.

The company paid for two trips home a month. The jet took off from Pensacola and landed at Panama City, Tampa, Orlando, Daytona, and finally Jacksonville. I felt like I was on a bus.

One night turbulence took over and my drink hung in mid air. A stewardess landed in a passenger's lap. The company chartered a plane for me to go to Palatka to get married. Howze was a great company for me at that time.

Buildings were appraised by the cost approach with comparable sales, if any, used as a check. Improved commercial should be appraised on the basis of income. A vacant building might be worthless.

Florida also taxes business equipment. Hard hit are restaurants and motels. Appraising a bed or French fry cooker is difficult.

Buy a Mobile Home

I became a project manager in Jackson County in Florida's panhandle, for Howze & Associates. At age 23, I was in charge of the re-appraisal for taxation in the entire county. The county seat was Marianna, a town of about 3,500. Linda pointed out that this rural county was full of prisons and mental institutions. I was thrilled to have the opportunity.

There was no place to live. Linda and I bought a new mobile home from a dealer in Pensacola, 100 miles to the west. I gave him a $100 post-dated check and they moved a 12 ft x 52 ft. two-bedroom unit and set it up on a rented lot. The lot rent was

$35 a month and the trailer cost $3,200, of which a finance company loaned us $3,100.

My boss arrived to help me hire workers. He turned down one lady because of her hairy legs. At the high point, I had 20 workers, mostly draftsmen. Land ownerships had to be drawn on aerial maps. I fired one particularly "assy" guy. I bought a 1966 Ford in Panama City, which aggravated the local dealer to no end. After doing appraising in Palatka, I felt qualified to do this little town.

The trailer was hot. I got a fan and wore no shirt. Linda and I got our first checks the same day. I made $6,000 a year and she made $4,000 as an elementary school teacher. We were two college graduates making a combined income of $10,000. We felt rich and bought a pile of clothes. We rented a row boat and paddled round one of the local lakes.

One hot night I noticed the unit shaking. It vibrated in a rhythmic way, would quit and then start again. The mystery was solved when I noticed the dachshund pacing up and down the hall.

Another night the president of the company visited us, after wrecking his car. I got to drive him around in my new Ford.

Like Dan Quayle, I was lucky to get into the Army Reserve. Six months after getting this job, I was called up for basic training. I sold the trailer, but the buyer was turned down by the finance company because he was an investor. I sold it again and told the finance company, "You'd better take this guy because I'm going off to serve my country."

Buy a Vandalized Estate from Your Relatives

Linda's family lived in East Palatka. Her grandmother lived in a cottage on the edge of Palatka. She died in 1966. Marge, Linda's mother had two sisters who lived out of state, so after grandmother died, no one was in charge and the house was vandalized.

It was a mess. There were holes in the walls and trash strewn everywhere. Someone had attacked the wiring. The toilet was stolen.

Dad acted as probate agent and got all the paperwork together so Linda and I could buy this place. We gave the heirs a note for $2,000 payable at $35 per month.

Dad and I set to work cleaning the place up. He liked physical work and I just took a picture of the fuse box. Linda got mad about this. We did no real repairs, just cosmetics. Picking up the trash and sweeping took a full day.

Three months later, Dad sold it for us. We held a note for $3,000 and received $50 a month. We got 6% interest and were only paying 4%.

The buyer was handy and had six kids. He made a porch into a living area and knocked out a wall between the porch and the bathroom, making the house total 900 sq. ft. He installed three toilets in the newly elongated bathroom.

Dad collected the mortgage money for us and told us about the bath. He sold the house twice and managed the collection for us, all for free.

Buy from Mad People

After being released from six months of Army training, I went back to work for Howze & Assoc. I helped Parker in the reappraisal of Screven County, Georgia. The town was Sylvania, 65 miles north of Savannah. It was 1967.

We lived in motels and drove home to Jacksonville every weekend. I joined a bottle club, since Screven was a dry county. The main restaurant had a parrot inside flying about, talking and squawking.

As in Pensacola, I appraised the land. The main road through downtown was U.S. 301. I valued a 30'x100' lot at $3,000. This was a commercial site and a low value due to poor size.

Book opening is the public hearing after all the appraising is done. The complaint sessions were long and difficult. We used no chairs except in the case of elderly or sick taxpayers.

A farmer in bib overalls said of his house, "It's got so many holes it looks like it's trying to breathe." An angry widow complained that she only had 300 acres. We had her down for 270. A man offered me a free house if I'd go easy on his other houses.

Mr. 30' came in mad as hell and he wasn't going to take it anymore! He slammed his file down and shouted, "It ain't worth $100!"

I stepped back and said, "Of course it's worth $100. It's worth $3,000 like it says." "No it ain't."

Parker whispered, "Buy it."

I got out my checkbook and said, "I'll give you $100." A blank deed was produced and 30' signed it in front of one of our notaries. I was gleeful; but my bank balance was only $15. Parker gave me his check for $200 and I signed the lot over to him.

Five years later, Parker sold the lot for $3,500, a return of 59% per annum.

Work for John Rogers

Rod Porter, a Palatka banker and friend, introduced me to John Rogers.

John had a house on Ortega Boulevard and the St. Johns River overlooking downtown Jacksonville. He bought it in the early 1960s for $75,000. Estimated value today is $2 million. I sat in his den and we talked.

A new MAI, Earl Miller, needed an assistant. I was hired to work for Earl. MAI stands for Member American Institute, the oldest appraisal society in America.

John and his brother, Henry, were old money and Earl was an eager, hard worker. I had prestige, too, in the form of Uncle Conrad who was known for his TV appearances in the late 1950's and early 1960's. Everywhere we went, John introduced me as R. Conrad Cooper's nephew.

It was 1968 and I was 25. I showed up at the six-story building in downtown Jacksonville before anyone else. I had no key my first day. Not to worry; I'd soon have lots of keys. John managed the building in return for reduced rent. John gave me a cigar box full of untagged keys and made me property manager for the firm. I never figured out what all the keys fit.

Soon I was looking into a toilet at Howard's Bar and dunning poachers on parking lots. Standing at a parking lot in freezing wind, I checked stickers and held out my hand to collect.

Earl had me looking up sales for his road right-of-way acquisition work. Most of his work was for the road department. I did a few houses. This was fee appraising, where you do an individual parcel rather than an entire community.

I had a private office which I filled with cigarette smoke. I dictated reports using a Grundig tape machine. Earl's secretary, Jackie, was a sexy thing but a church-goer. Earl tithed and didn't cuss or drink.

Vickie was John's secretary. She was a flashy blonde who wore silver mini-skirts. John was very proper, but he liked to show her off. She worked on her own schedule.

Earl and John, also an MAI, got some great appraisals. I helped do a bank, warehouse, a subdivision and got loads of experience.

John wanted to have coffee every morning, but we got too busy for that. John and Henry understood that my main job was helping Earl; but one day John said, "Jeff, please take my car and pick up Peachman at the airport." Hot damn, I thought, I get to drive John's car. But all he had was an older Chevrolet.

Peachman took the entire sixth floor in more ways than one. John paid a fortune to have partitions moved and Peachy moved in a telephone boiler room crew and began selling shares in non-existent peach orchards.

Peach knew he was going to leave town and quit paying rent. Finally John booted his door. An iron cover was installed over the knob and we had the only key. Finally Peachy was jailed.

Earl's and my life changed when we talked to Charter Mortgage. Charter was a mortgage banker, among other things and they placed big loans for life insurance companies.

The appraisals had to be inflated about 20% above value so the client could get a 100% loan. We didn't sign the reports. They paid well and I got to travel to other states.

Charter bragged that they had never had a foreclosure. Back then, inflation bailed out all but the worst deals. I taught several of them how to do the appraisals and they taught me how to drink at lunch.

When I set up on my own, not one Charter job came my way. This was one of the biggest surprises of my young life. I took a different road instead, one to Putnam County.

Charter went bankrupt after the recession of 1974. Earl gave up his license after being tainted by a jailed developer in 1991. Vickie opened a popular restaurant called The Wine Cellar. John and Henry are still in the real estate business, but not together.

Buy a VA Repossession

The Veterans Administration has a 100% of value loan program. If buyers fail to make the payments, the VA ends up owning the house, so they have a lot of houses. The prices are cheap, but not negotiable.

In 1969, I felt my job with Rogers was solid and so was Linda's as a teacher. We rode the Holiday Hill area and found an FHA repo to buy; but it was on the lottery system and another buyer got it.

Next we found a nice fixed up VA repo and bought the block rancher on Altama Road for $14,200. You don't have to be a veteran to buy a VA repossession. Payments were made to the U.S. Treasury.

The house had fresh paint and gleaming parquet floors. Parquet is wood squares. There were three bedrooms and two baths. There was central heat, but no air. The drawback to the house was a tiny kitchen.

I didn't think we needed termite protection because the house was concrete block. Then one day I came home to a swarm of insects eating the woodwork.

We decided on Sears for central air conditioning. It cost $1,000 to have a condenser added. Everything else was already in place. They ran the drain through the slab and into the dirt. The house flooded so they came back and ran the drain outside.

The oil heat belched black smoke out the ducts and insurance paid for some of that damage. We had the kitchen refinished, but it was still small.

During this time, Stephanie was born. She was two when we divorced. In 1971, I got the house and sold it for $18,600. I got rid of the $105 a month house payment and moved into a $300 a month apartment. I also bought a new red car.

Twenty eight years later, the house is worth $75,000, a return of 6% per annum. Buy a repaired lender-owned house in a good neighborhood to live in.

One definition of a good deal is: Can you sell it right away for profit?

Buy a Cheap, Well Located Apartment

John Rogers started the Jacksonville Multiple Listing Service in 1965. This is the system where Realtors share their listings and prospects to improve the market for real estate. There was one listing (property for sale) per page and each week the book was updated by hand. Today it is a website.

I was putting in new listings in 1968 and saw a three-unit apartment for $10,500. The two-story frame building was built as an apartment with two units down and one up. It had 1,500 sq. ft. and was near downtown. The building was old then, but located one lot off a busy road, one block off the St. Johns River, and you could see tall buildings in the distance.

I barely knew how to fill out a purchase offer. I paid the full price, but with only $1,000 down and the seller holding the balance. There was no existing mortgage to get in the way. I was lucky and checked the right box. Since the seller paid the commission and termite damage, he had to bring cash to the closing, since I was only investing $1,000.

Ken Richman, Roger's employee, saw my purchase and hooted, "You paid $10,500 for THAT?" Years later my parents rode by a house I had bought in Palatka and said, "That's just a Jim Walter."

After opening my office in 1970, I needed money. Cash, a friend I met in the Army Reserve, was loaded with money and bought the apartment from me. I sold the apartment to Cash for $12,500 and sold it again later for him for $14,500. I created value when I bought the unit for the low down payment and assumable mortgage. I also caught the crest of inflation. The apartment was a good deal for me because it created activity and I made commissions. I made other sales from the people I met showing that property.

Clean Up and Get Noticed

Ken Richman founded Appreciation Corporation. He modeled it after one of Roger's companies. I bought $100 worth of stock.

Ken was the son of a well-respected minister and had access to the church roster. He also went to medical conventions. Ken was a smooth talker and had an excellent pool of investors. Appreciation was capitalized at $50,000. I talked my future landlord, Meadows, into buying $1,000 worth of stock.

Appreciation bought a brick two-story, four-unit apartment for $20,000 in 1969. It backed up to the 20th Street Expressway and fronted on 21st Street. It was across from a medium rise office building which was owned by Volkswagen. Ken put $5,000 down on the tenantless building.

The younger and poorer members of Appreciation met at the apartment to fix it up. There I was, holding a paint brush. I felt a sense of hopelessness at the drop in the bucket effort we were making. I looked ahead at dozens of weekends going up in smoke.

Ken either wasn't there or dressed up for a business meeting somewhere.

Volkswagen noticed the activity. They decided to buy before we got the building filled with tenants. Six months after our purchase, they paid $40,000 for the apartment, tore it down and used the lot for parking. That's a return of 147% per annum.

Fueled by success, Ken bought an old store cross the street from a proposed high rise addition for Blue Cross Insurance. Ken had not seen the plans. When the 20-story addition was built, our store looked directly into the garbage dumpster pit, which was noisily unloaded twice daily.

We sold for a loss. Do not mistake good luck for brains. You cannot replicate a real estate deal. Each one is and must be different, if for no other reason than location.

Buy from Rich People Because They Don't Need the Money

In 1969 I decided to open my own office and knew I would need a good location. I saw a classified ad: "150 ft. on Beach

Blvd., $1,000 down." Low down payments make things happen! The seller was Dr. Gain, whose office was next door to the property. His surplus corner had four-lane frontage and a traffic light. The improvements were two old frame houses. I could fix up the front one for my office and rent out the back one.

I met Dr. Gain at his home on the St. Johns River in Mandarin, south of Jacksonville. We went for a ride in his boat. Dr. Gain said, "Everyone should live on the river." The doctor liked me because I was young and energetic. I liked him because he was rich. Real estate contracts can be very personal. Dr. Gain wanted $45,000 for the corner, top dollar at the time, but he didn't want the money now. The last thing he needed was to pay more income taxes. He would retire in 12 years and would want it then. I could take over the first mortgage and use the property and not pay him a nickel for 12 years. Then he would receive an income from the second mortgage, which would then be a first mortgage.

Great though the deal was, I couldn't afford it. The contractor's bid to renovate the front house was $3,500, way beyond my budget. John Meadows, a real estate investor, had offered me a small office in his building for $75 per month. Dr.

Gain was holding my $100 earnest money deposit. I had only 30 days to close or lose the $100.

I showed John Rogers the option-contract and said, "Buy this." John knew the power of those terms and he liked the commercial, one-third-acre corner property. John gave me $500 for my $100 option.

Dr. Gain felt cheated when John, not me, turned out to be the buyer. I explained that John had real financial strength and $45,000 was top dollar for his corner! I convinced the doctor with comparable sales that the sale to Rogers was far better than letting it fall through, and he closed the sale. I felt pretty smart turning $100 into $500 in 30 days.

The property has grown from $45,000 to $180,000 over 29 years which is only 4.9% per annum. Suburban streets may stagnate while growth occurs further out or in totally new areas.

I bought and sold to rich people with whom I had a personal relationship. The buyer, a Realtor, understood the complicated financing and was a noted nothing-down investor.

The First Five Years in My Own Business

On February 1, 1970 Jeff Cooper Company, not incorporated, opened for business in the Meadows Building on the Arlington Expressway, Jacksonville, Florida.

Linda and I hosted an opening party. My banker, Rod, was there. He had loaned me $2,500 to get started. I had suspected that my credit ability came from my parents. Rod knew they would bail me out and he knew that Conrad would bail them out. Years later, I used plastic instead of real bankers.

After the party was over, I felt fear. What now? Soon salesmen were lined up. I bought a check-writer, postage machine and refrigerator. I justified the refrigerator based on lunches eaten in the office. Soon a customer came in while I was eating a sandwich so that idea ended.

John Rogers hired me to rent the two houses he had acquired from Dr. Gain. He said, "Rent them cheap and make it clear we do no repairs."

I ran an ad: house for rent $100 month, half of market rent at that time. A flood of people showed up. I talked so much that hoarseness set in. They both rented in one day and John sent me a letter of congratulations. I forgot about them for a time.

Dad and I pressured Linda to get a real estate license to help me out. This was a mistake. Linda didn't want to work for me. She didn't even want me to have this business.

I worked like hell. I advertised other broker's listings since I had few of my own. Despite progress and Linda's income as a teacher, I still could see the end of my money.

Then Dad called. He could get me a trailer park appraisal which paid a fee of $75. I was there the next morning. The "park" was in East Palatka and had only five spaces. It took a long time to collect the fee. How typical this was. Still, that job kicked off my career. I was to do Putnam County appraisals for the next 20 years. I was the only trained appraiser serving Palatka for all of the 1970s.

I got on the FHA panel in Jacksonville. FHA is the Federal Housing Administration. FHA's paid $25. The one page form could be filled out in pencil. I could do four in one day, and that was big money.

My appraisal career began by accident. I had no idea there was such a demand in Putnam County. Dad's popularity and my competence were a winning combination.

One of Roger's renters didn't pay, so I stopped by. The den (former carport) had flooded. It had been that way for months. They just splashed around in it, afraid to call me. Thank God no one was electrocuted. The other house became vacant, my first. Four college students lived there. They saved all their pop bottles. Millions of roaches now inhabited the house. It was like the movie *"Joe's Apartment."*

My associates sold a few houses, but for the most part I had land listings. They were less demanding than home sales and did not result in any conflict of interest with appraisal. We specialized in small residential and commercial land parcels. Some were on the water, abundant in Jacksonville,

Dad and I incorporated together in 1973. Prior to that, my secretary did my books and my taxes were a mess. I was audited twice and had to pay for excess mileage deduction. I was constantly bombarded with surprise tax payments and a borrowing pattern began.

My personal sales experiences were chaotic. Once I was driving to an appointment to show a house. I was late and traffic was heavy. A little English Ford was in front, blocking me from real speed. Finally a break came and I floored my Olds Cutlass. The powerful eight-cylinder rear wheel drive car fishtailed and spewed debris all on the Ford. When I got to the house, no one was there. Shit, I thought, he's been here and left. I was checking the house for locked doors when the old English Ford drove up and stopped.

Worse than that was manning open houses. One place I was sitting had multicolored shag carpet and a paneled kitchen. I was pacing, sweating and waiting when a young couple walked in and loved the house. They bought it the next day.

Buying a home is very stressful. One guy's wife flirted with me and another wife started crying over the wallpaper. Another time a baby threw up in the back seat of my car. A drunk wanted to look at homes. I found out he did this every weekend for enjoyment.

The oil embargo of 1974 changed my life. The market for land dried up. Not only were buyers scared in general, but who would buy land if there was no gas to get to it?

I quit getting listings and concentrated on appraisals. It was more steady and had lower overhead. When the VA appointment came, my appraisal future was set. Unlike the FHA which came and went, the VA was steady and professional. Jacksonville is a big Navy town and VA appraisals made me rich, or so it seemed.

Great and Humble Homes

Word spread quickly that I was appraising in Putnam County, since there was a great need for this in 1971.

Palatka Federal Savings and Loan Association hired me at $45 per report on the condition that I got two a day.

Ben Strode was the staff appraiser who handed out the work. He'd talk to me about each case and the president of the bank, Jim Millican, would pep me up on the difficult ones. Word spread that I was "bank approved" and all kinds of work came in, commercial and residential. My fee went up. For $45 they got no comparable sales.

I saw some homes 1'd never see any other way. One was two-story, down a dirt road on a lake. It was Spanish style and had elaborate interior columns. It was being bought by a man from Israel for $50,000. The two owners of the furniture factory each owned elaborate mansions on the river in Palatka. They had Grecian columns and guest houses. They became estates and were run down, but still stately. Another place like this was sold and the buyer put a brick front on it.

Down from Dad's house was a three-story with turret. It was cut up into apartments and then restored back to a residence. Another three-story with tower had stained glass and beautiful wood. Another river view home was moved out of Palatka.

In 1971 Dad and I bid on 24 city blocks to be acquired by the Urban Renewal Agency. We worked with Frank George, architect. Most of the homes were low income minority occupied. About half were owned and half rented. There were some commercial properties, too, along U.S. 17 or Reid St.

I spend a full day bidding the job. The price to complete in four months was $17,000. We sent letters announcing the time of our coming inspection. My tax appraisal experience came in handy with this work. We set up an assembly line and hired a local young man to help. Dad and I divided the fee with $10,000 to me and $7,000 to him.

Many houses were cleaned up for us. These people did not want a government program. They were happy with their paint-less homes.

We didn't worry about crime back then. A tall white sheriff with a long barreled pistol walked the streets of "colored town." He was The Law and whatever he did went unquestioned.

1971 was my first complete year in my own business and I felt rich, but money was tight. I had to borrow to live until the big fee came in. I also resigned from the FHA panel to do this job and was never able to get back on it

We finished on time, but the project was canceled. No sites were acquired. We got paid, but did all that for nothing.

Big jobs hurt cash flow and in my case ruptured other tender parts of life.

Putnam Appraisals

One of Dad's first appraisals was big, setting values for lands flooded by the new Cross-Florida Barge Canal, under construction in 1965. This canal was touted as saving shipping the long trip around the Keys, but was closed halfway through construction for environmental reasons. The Cross Florida Barge Canal would have been 185 miles long and 150' wide at its bottom. The fear was salt water intrusion into Florida's groundwater table. President Johnson started the canal and President Nixon ended it.

During college I'd help Dad write his appraisal reports. He turned them over to me as soon as possible. I kept files in a three ring binder. Many of the appraisals were sales and served as comparables for future jobs.

We did an eel farm, Indian mound, funeral home, peach orchard, church camp, ferns, apartments, commercial, industrial, trailers, hotels, etc.

George Hall was a powerful banker in Green Cove Springs and Palatka. He owned 13 mostly run-down buildings on St. Johns

Ave., Palatka's main shopping street.   He rode up and down the street in a yellow Cadillac, wearing a 3 piece suit and derby hat. In 1968, Dad and another broker were appointed by the court to appraise his estate.   Howze & Associates and I had just appraised downtown Palatka.   They valued 2nd floor space at 60% of first floor value even though most upper floors were vacant and worthless.   Dad and Joe added 20% on top of the already too high values.   I was paid $250 or ¼ of the fee to write, type and assemble the report.   When the properties didn't sell, the heirs became angry.   The cost approach is inappropriate for old buildings.   Here, the income approach should have been used.

Southpork owned a five-acre fish camp with multiple buildings. He had no survey and I examined several maps to estimate the five acres. This was in 1975; my $300 bill went unpaid.

Southpork insisted his camp was seven acres. He had stepped it off. I offered to change the report if he could get a survey, but he refused. If he had only five acres he didn't want to know.

I went to small claims court and got a judgment. 12 years later he sold the camp. The interest ran at 12% so my fee was now $600. Like Dad said, "Money don't spoil."

The slaughter house appraisal was in July. Many large buildings occupied an entire Palatka city block. I did the outside first and then felt relief at the relative cool inside. I saw the hog tied at the feet swing in on conveyor rope. Then I saw a black man in rubber coat with large knife. I looked away, but heard the squeal.

I measured a sawmill and stepped in a hole. It had rained and sawdust was floating over the hole so it was invisible.

During the tax reappraisal, I counted fireplaces while the paper mill was appraised on the back of a napkin over cocktails.

One deranged client had a jail inside his house. Many jobs happened when the government had a 3% loan program. An old three-story hotel got renovated into office space: a daring and successful project.

Many Putnam jobs were repeats. The client had added something and wanted a bigger loan.

Robert Browning was the first client I refused to work for. This brash developer was eventually arrested for land fraud.

I lost the Seminole Electric right of way job to Roy Black even though his bid was three times higher than mine. The FBI investigated Seminole and Black faced jail on another job later on.

Dad helped me do these jobs. We'd ride 20 miles down a dirt road to appraise a cheap house and get stuck. By 1980 Dad had angina, but still helped me push the car. I'd buy aerial maps to help find the property. Once we got lost and a man pulled a pistol. I stated our business, but he was no help and we left promptly.

The ranch was over 500 acres. The owner was showing us around and I had to ask, "Don't these flies bother you?"

He drawled, "Yeah, when they are bad."

A log truck lost its load and blocked me in for over two hours.

Dad did leg work for me and his secretary Eunice went after slow paying clients, of which there were many. I made a little money selling data to other appraisers.

After Max Gilbert bought the 1/3 acre taxi stand, he had plans drawn for a luxurious two-story office building. I was to appraise it. Palatka had never seen anything like this and comparables were scarce. I applied several creative techniques and valued it highly. A Miami bank called with all sorts of criticisms about guidelines, etc. Insulted, I hung up on him. Max must have talked to him because he called back sweet as sugar. I redid the report, but the edifice was never built.

I have collected an impressive file of photographs covering the many appraisals. Putnam has many beautiful lakes and rivers.

One day I was complaining about a particularly tough assignment and Dad, beaming with pride, said, "They pick you for the hard jobs." No wonder he was good at selling real estate.

Palatka Greats

B. A. Wilkes was a Palatka real estate investor. He owned a city block and would build a store for a good tenant. He had some known tenants such as Dollar Store. Over a long time period he built five stores or offices on that block. Dad and I helped him with appraisals and information.

B. A. and his wife lived in a large ranch house on the hill on Crill Avenue. She got a new '57 Chrysler New Yorker and came by our apartment to show it to Mother. It was white with dark blue interior and when she put the electric window down, cold air rushed out of the car. I was astounded. They seemed above us socially, but we had something they didn't: Conrad.

Whenever Conrad and Irene came to Palatka we'd all eat at the Wilkes'. Usually Conrad's visit made the paper and he'd go to Kiwanis with Dad.

I still admire the way B. A. built his block. He helped the town and himself with careful management and creativity.

Another interesting guy was Joe Carlin. He ran an ice cream shop until he got into home building. He joined other businessmen and created many new block ranch homes on the edge of Palatka. He had a nice home on the river in East Palatka. His daughter was too beautiful for me to date. He had the only swimming pool I knew of in high school.

Max Gilbert liked owning Palatka real estate and was quite a promoter. His idea of rents was New York rents. He was a very skilled borrower of money and I spoke on his behalf at a zoning meeting and later testified against him at a zoning trial.

Mitchell owned low income units, stores and a lumber mill. All went into decline and I also appraised their beach condo. Many Palatka greats have ocean front houses or condominiums. Their favorite beach was Crescent Beach south of St. Augustine.

Frank George was an architect with whom we worked on Urban Renewal projects. He built for his family a beautiful lake front house. This house had style and grace. It was geometrically intricate, but tasteful.

George Miller founded Miller Enterprises, a grocery and convenience store chain. They were one of my biggest clients. They are headquartered in Crescent City, a little town south of Palatka and on Crescent Lake, connected to the St. Johns River by Dunn's Creek. Thus, if you live on this lake, you can navigate to the Atlantic Ocean.

George had a grocery store and strip center in Crescent City. I appraised this in 1995 and thought, "One of the secrets of his success is that he puts a grocery store in a town so small that it never has any competition." Like Wal-Mart.

Conway owned hundreds of low income rentals in Palatka. They all looked the same, simulated brick tar paper. This investment is management intensive. Daily collections and repairs are required. Did he trade repairs for rent? Probably. He knew all his tenant's names and situations. He was a father figure and the law was on his side.

He was a "benevolent dictator" who did a good job and a job most people couldn't do. He was rich and would count his money every weekend on the dining room table. His son went to our school and had a hot-rod.

I appraised his estate pre-death for gifting to his heirs. I got confused over some of the addresses and he said some of the houses had been moved, but the numbers were not changed. He was willful, cranky, but honest and fair.

Angel's Dining Car on US 17 was popular when I was a boy, and 60 years later it is a tourist attraction. They have great cheap food and a cracked window.

Sell Before You Have to Put in Bathrooms

In the early 1970s, I made the trip from Jacksonville to Palatka almost once a week. Once there I'd often drive another hour or two getting to various appraisals. I'd socialize with Dad, Mother and sales associates. I'd learn about and advise on deals pending.

Paul Hege, manager of the J. C. Penney department store in downtown Palatka, was social and knew many people. He retired from Penney's to become Dad's sales associate. The store was later moved out to the mall on the edge of town.

Mitch owned 10 low income duplexes. They were paintless buildings on blocks and had tin roofs and outside toilets. The yards were mostly sand and under the porches were dogs that hated white people.

Mitch, claiming poor health, said to Paul, "Please get me out of this; I'11 take anything." The salesman is often the first to know of a good deal before it ever hits the general market.

Paul said, "How low will you go?" They settled on a price of $20,000 or only $1,000 per rental unit. They were all full.

Palatka never had any shortage of poor people. The rent was about $500 a year per unit. He'd have the investment back in two years. Paul knew the land was worth $20,000, so how could he lose?

Soon after Paul closed on this deal, the city required all houses to have inside toilets, showers or baths. I think Mitch knew this was coming, but hey, it was still a good deal. Paul set about installing showers as they were cheaper than tubs. He spent $5,000 and a lot of backbreaking work on bathrooms.

Some tenants still used the outside toilets and hung clothes in the showers so Paul had to haul the privies to the dump. Paul was not discouraged and bought more rental property.

Low grade houses require a lot of ongoing maintenance.

Buy before the Building Permit is Available

In 1972, Dad bought a strip of land sandwiched between the railroad and State Road 100 on the edge of Palatka. The parcel was 30' by 1,500' and he paid $100 for it. A month later, he sold the strip for $1,000. Five years later the railroad abandoned their tracks. The rail land was 100' wide and now surplus. The land agent contacted each adjacent owner about buying that part next to them.

Dad's buyer paid the railroad $4,500 for the 100' by 1,500' parcel. This represented the going rate at that time of $1,000 per acre.

Dad's buyer now had 130' x 1,500' of four-lane highway frontage, enough to get a building permit. In fact, the buyer eventually parceled out six sales totaling $150,000. Several commercial buildings were constructed by the various new owners. This represented a return of 34% per annum over 10 years.

Assemblage or plottage value occurs when parcels are combined to achieve a greater value than separately. Usually the shape or utility is increased. Setback laws may render a site unbuildable, but when combined with its neighbor, the new site is a powerhouse.

The strip of 30' x 1,500' totals 45,000 sq. ft. which is 1.03 acres. An acre is defined as any parcel of land totaling 43,560 sq. ft. A square acre is about 209' x 209'. Not all acres are created equal.

Buy corporate surplus before the building permit is available.

Make a Lake

John Rogers had an exciting office and he didn't seem to work hard. He and investors created Asbury Realty, which owned a new lake. Florida has so many lakes that I couldn't understand at first why you would make one.

South of Jacksonville in Clay County is Black Creek. This meandering creek can flood as topography changes rapidly. The key tool was topographic maps or contour maps made by the government and sold for just a few dollars each. Changes in land elevation are marked on the map in five foot intervals.

Rogers and Tom Ryan found a unique parcel. It contained five fingers draining into Black Creek and the elevation invited a dam. The earth dam cost $50,000 and the water backed up, making miles of lake frontage. Then they platted a subdivision know as Lake Asbury and sold waterfront and back lots.

Tom was a Methodist minister and real estate salesman. He lived on site and was head broker. Asbury held the paper in typical Florida fashion—15 year payouts. The roads were graded except for one paved state road.

Insurance companies were reluctant to cover houses on dirt roads in this remote location. Crime also occurred. Tom was a brilliant salesman and overcame all this in time. Deed restrictions required that good quality homes be built.

Roads were named for religious people and a Methodist Church was built. Gradually, the population grew down to Lake Asbury and the development was no longer remote. Roads were improved. The dam was strengthened.

This development began in 1964 and was a daring success. It would be illegal today because of environmental laws; but the early buyers have been richly rewarded.

Tom performed the ceremony when Martha and I married in 1974, and he also married her daughter, Kelli, to Steve.

Buy Lake Land

One of my first Putnam appraisals was 40 acres with a completely contained 20-acre lake within that land. There was a house, too. I wanted to own an entire lake.

A key issue is whether or not the water level is stable. Keystone Heights, south of Jacksonville, has many beautiful lakes but water levels fell to record lows. Docks were left on dry land and in one case a developer actually sold more lots on newly exposed land.

Lake land may contain muck which could render the land unbuildable unless the muck is removed or pilings set in it to reach firm ground. This could easily cost more than the land is worth. A surveyor or engineer can take test borings of the soil.

Examine topographic maps or contour maps, because rising water can wipe out most (if not all) of your land. I appraised a lake parcel and examined two topographic maps, one from 1975 and one from 1935. In 1935, the land was completely covered by lake water. Shrinking water levels seem to be the norm.

Buy with the cottage already there. If not, make your purchase contingent upon getting a building permit, which will hinge on the availability of septic tanks and wells.

Florida has a 10% set aside law for commercial land development. This 10% must be in a pond to catch storm water runoff and aid in pollution control. This results in some bizarre sights. Some are beautifully landscaped and some are ringed in concrete to look like open sewers.

Subdivisions have lakes to comply with the 10% set aside law and to aid in drainage. In some cases, flood zones are alleviated. Developers charge more for lake lots, but they can be worth less. Drainage clogs may flood your lot, grass may fill the lake or it could dry up.

Engineered lakes allow you to see dozens of other home rears, some of which may look bad or have crummy fencing. Alligators can breed, as well as mosquitoes and flies.

Generally, lake projects have held value better than non-lake projects, other things being equal.

Borrow pits can have steep drop offs or pollution. These are dug for new construction such as interstate highways.

From Ponds to Apartments

The Bunnells were from Wisconsin, but bought 300 acres near Hudson Pulp and Paper north of Palatka. The land had dozens of ponds for raising shiners or minnows for fishing. The Bunnells sold these fishes to camp operators like my father.

I worked at the mill during summers, off from college. They paid $2.45 an hour, an unbelievable sum back in 1963. That was union wage, but they moved me every 30 days so I couldn't join. I worked in every department at the mill, about 30. Some of those jobs were dangerous and we frequently pulled double shifts.

The mill had 3,500 employees in 1961. I could see the labor saving devices that were abandoned. In 1991, I did an appraisal for the mill and while the physical plant had expanded, the employees were down to 1,800---union or not.

In 1964, the mill bought Bunnells' 300 acres. They changed the use of the land from shiner hatchery to sewage dump. The ponds were ideal for dumping waste and excess chemicals. They paid a premium price too, $10,000 per acre or $300,000 total.

The Bunnells then moved to Jacksonville and bought apartments, about 30 units. Super inflation hit in the 1970s and they got rich a second time. Bill Watson, Realtor, handled the sales.

Know the Seller and Make a Low Offer

While with Rogers in 1969, I listed Fudd's Restaurant site at Cassat Ave. and Interstate 10, a pin location in Jacksonville. "Pin" means first on or off the interchange ramp. It was a big site about 100' x 400' and priced at $135,000. I looked up what Fudd paid and it was $115,000 in 1966.

Rogers allowed me to take this listing with me when I set up on my own. For $50 I had Dell Signs put up a 4' x 8' Jeff Cooper Co. sale sign. It was great advertising. I got calls, but no sale resulted. The file grew inches thick. I visited Fudd's home office in Ohio and got minimal acknowledgment. The site was important to me, but not to Fudd.

Fudd built a restaurant on another site. This closed after a few years and was bought by Rolls, who turned it into a show bar, the Pink Lady.

My written listing ran out and they refused to renew, but I continued working on an open basis, although not very hard. Open listing means first come, first served, with the commission, if any going to the performing broker.

Hemp, a carpet dealer saw my sign and wanted to make an offer. We wrote up a contract for $95,000. Hemp knew Rolls and said, "Let's go over to the Pink Lady for lunch." Rolls said, "$95,000 is bullshit. I know these people. Watch this." Rolls picked up the telephone and bought the site for $80,000 cash, fast closing. Hemp tore up my contract. Rolls assigned his rights to Hemp.

Hemp and I drove back to his car and he said, "Don't worry, I'll take care of you." A month went by and Hemp called, "Come get your check." I drove over to a high rise apartment on the river and took the elevator to the penthouse. Hemp gave me a check for $4,000. I had no rights in this deal, but Hemp had a conscience.

Fudd paid $115,000 in 1966 and sold for $80,000 in 1973. Appraisals justified both transactions. The real estate man looks good as long as an appraisal is in file higher than the purchase price and lower than the sale price. I spent about half my money at the Pink Lady, but it did not help. The place burned and arson was suspected.

Buy Washed-out Oceanfront

When I was with Rogers, I met Mr. Williams, who was a stock broker down the hall. He had a young assistant, Jim Radcliffe, who became one of my friends. One of my first listings after opening my office in 1970 belonged to Mr. Williams.

Neptune Beach at Jacksonville was hard hit by Hurricane Dora in 1964. My listing was a washed out ocean front lot 50' x 100' but with only 10' of land left at the roadside. The price was $5,000. I hammered a sign and looked at this opportunity with pride.

Comparables indicated that only two lots like this had sold since Hurricane Dora. One for $1,800 and another $2,000. Beach

Realtors implied that I was unethical for taking an overpriced listing. I still believed in the listing, but was uneducated about how long it took to sell land. I dreamed of spending $500 (10%) right away.

One year went by and I had all but forgotten about this listing. Roger's brother Henry knew a doctor who wanted the lot and submitted an offer for $4,750 cash. Mr. Williams accepted and the sale closed. My commission was now 5% after paying Henry Rogers.

Years later the Corps of Engineers raised the beach level by dumping sand from the ocean. The doctor brought in fill of his own and the lot became level and buildable. Over 25 years the value rose to $200,000, which is a return of 15% per annum.

Buy a Jail

By 1972 the old Palatka city jail was outmoded. A grand new jail was built on the St. Johns River by the bridge. The old jail was a nondescript stucco building on a 50' x 100' lot. It was only two blocks from Dad's office. The jail was on a side street between

St. Johns Ave., the main local street, and U. S. 17 or Reid St., the main road through Palatka. It was, of course, full of iron bars.

The city offered the jail by open bid. There were no bidders. Dad looked up the tax assessment (appraised value) - $1,370, which is what he offered. The city could hardly argue with its own appraisal and since there were no other bidders, Dad got the jail!

I was thrilled to own a jail. Too bad I didn't have a badge. Dad had no use for it, but it was near property he owned. He swept it clean and the abutting owner on U. S. 17 noticed the activity. He paid Dad $2,400 for the jail 30 days later in order to expand backward.

Despite this quick profit, Dad kicked himself for years because he felt it was an excellent long term investment. The new owner tore the building down and removed the iron bars.

By 1990, the river jail was torn down. The asbestos problem really complicated the demolition. A super mammoth jail was built on the edge of town. The river jail lot is available for development.

Buy government surplus. They feel pressure to get rid of it so private owners can start paying taxes on it. The government has no stake in getting full value, but they don't want bad publicity from selling too cheaply either. Sometimes government will wholesale property if it will bring in jobs and new construction.

Buy Well Located Oceanfront

Ken Richman, was the owner of Appreciation Corp. In 1971 Ken bought the map of South Ponte Vedra oceanfront. He looked up the names of all owners and contacted them. He bought a total of five lots for $5,000 each. South Ponte Vedra is south of Jacksonville Beach. There were not many houses back then. The lots were big at 75' x 150' each. They were well elevated with tight vegetation cover. They fronted paved State Road A1A, a two-lane highway.

The Federal Flood Insurance program was created and expensive homes began to be built. Hindsight proves we sold these lots far too soon and too cheaply, but I was anxious to broker the lots and get a commission. I held stock in Appreciation and had set up on my own. Some members complained about the too quick turnover, but we sold four of the lots for $7,500 and the last one was sold to Dr. Cuba for $9,000.

Dr. Cuba was a pathologist who loved to drink beer. I had a few with him, but was still able to fill out the contract. At the last minute he got worried that I might be a fraud so he looked me up in the phone book. At that time I had a big ad with a picture of the Meadows' Building in it. He was satisfied.

Two years later we sold Dr. Cuba a 4,000 sq. ft. house in town. The bank loaned him the mortgage and the down payment. Twenty-five years after we bought the ocean lots, they appreciated to $150,000 each or a return of 14% per annum.

Buy Eroding Oceanfront before it is Bulk-headed

In 1972, I received a mailer on an ocean lot for sale in Fernandina Beach, Nassau County, Florida. This is north of Jacksonville and is now the home of Amelia Island Plantation Resort, a nationally known recreational community. The lot was

100' by 200' and priced reasonably at $15,000. I could buy it for $2,500 down and the balance held by the seller. Low down payments always got me going.

I took a girlfriend with me for the inspection. We walked over the land and I impressed her with my ability to buy and knowledge about oceanfront. Upon leaving I noticed that the two right wheels had left the hard road and became buried in the soft shoulder. I dug the car out, sweating and cussing.

I called the South Florida broker's agent handling the sale and bought it over the phone. The agent said sorry, but his broker sold it over the weekend. "Don't worry, I have another one just like it."

The contract arrived in the mail and it said: "Buyer is aware of and accepts the erosion problem." I hadn't noticed any erosion problem. I went back and looked up maps in the courthouse. The plat was filed in 1925 and at the time the lots were 300' deep. The land lost 100' of depth over a 47-year period. I let the deal drop. I knew too much.

The Corps of Engineer brought in granite riprap and promptly stopped any erosion problem for now. Many fine homes have been built since 1972. The land appreciated to $175,000 over 24 years or 10.3% per annum.

Buy Oceanfront Next to a Friend

Herb Scheidel was an encyclopedia sales manager. He had a good year in 1967 and received a large bonus. He bought an oceanfront house in Neptune Beach for $26,000.

Herb was single by 1971, as was I. I visited him at the new digs and thought; this is the life for me.

1973 was a good year for me. The DOW hit 1,000 for the first time and anything was possible. I bought a Porsche.

Herb's neighbor, Grease, called and said he wanted to sell his house. It was next to Herb's and similar to it. The block home was about 1,400 sq. ft. and filled most of the lot. I gave Grease a $1,200 non-refundable deposit on a $50,000 cash price. I was confident about getting the loan I needed to close.

Blue, my mortgage man, had also assured me, "No problem." Later, I learned that a mortgage man saying, "No problem" is the same as a doctor saying, "Bend over." I submitted my papers to Blue and waited. I waited some more. Finally Blue said, "I'm sorry, but we are not interested." I had run out of time and lost the $1,200 deposit.

I needed about $25,000 to put down. Lenders look on oceanfront as risky. Inflation was so high then that I had tried to peddle the contract. A year later we sold Grease's house and a vacant lot beside it for $75,000. My lost deposit came back in the form of a commission, except that Grease stole the refrigerator.

Buy a Run-down Store, Fix It Up and Move In

After Dad sold his two plots on the edge of Palatka, he wanted an office in town. In 1968 he assembled 1/3 acre on St. Johns Ave., the main local street. There was a taxi stand 10' by 15'. Dad loved low overhead and made that his office.

Across the street was a dilapidated store at the corner of St. Johns Ave. and 9th St. This five-bay place had 5,000 sq. ft. It badly needed a roof, but still one tenant hung on, Mary Carter Paints.

Dad was cramped in the taxi stand and he couldn't have an associate. He looked at the store across the street every day for months. He went inside the store and discovered leaks and fallen ceiling.

The property was paid for, so there was no existing mortgage to get in the way. Dad offered $18,000 for the store with $500 down and balance seller held at 4%, payable $100 a month. Mary Carter paid rent of $85 a month, so this was a safe deal.

Dad was handy and he bought hundreds of sheets of corrugated steel and a barrel of tar. He had never replaced a roof, but proceeded vigorously. It was hot work and he was then 68 years old. He paid as he went and a year later the building was clean and all bays rented save one.

Dad was a laid back manager. He never raised a rent and if a tenant was late he'd say, "Money don't spoil." He got four checks a month and said, "Better than a jab with a sharp stick."

In 1973 Dad sold me the store for $35,000, nothing down. I assumed the first mortgage and gave Dad a second mortgage for $18,000. Mary Carter got worried that I would sell, so I offered him a lease at $100 a month and he declined.

Six months later I did sell, to Max Gilbert, a Jacksonville contractor. He paid $45,000 to me. I pocketed $10,000 in cash and Dad collected on the $18,000 second mortgage. I spent my cash but Dad received $165 a month for 13 years totaling $25,000. Max also bought Dad's taxi stand.

Max raised all rents to $250 per month. A stunned Mary Carter moved out, as did everyone else. Max also ripped off Dad's roof and installed his own including a mansard front. High vacancy didn't bother Max.

Over five years the value of the property went from $18,000 to $45,000, which is 18.5% per annum minus the re-roofing work. Dad always valued his time low. It is almost impossible to figure a rate of return on real estate.

This is a good example of Dad and I working together for our mutual benefit.

Rent to Get Your Foot in the Door

We needed a place to move after Max's tremendous rent increase. Two blocks to the east was a dilapidated two-bay store. It was full of junk and paid the out of state owner no rent. The lot was 25' by 150' and the building was 25' by 50'. The owner, Dr. Finley, lived in Washington D.C. He wouldn't sell, but he would lease. Dad rented the junked-filled property for five years at $125 a month. He and his associate Paul began cleaning it. Dad was only 73 then. Paul hung paneling and in all, they spent $2,000 on improvements.

We moved our real estate office into one bay and rented the other bay for $125 a month. After getting back the $2,000, we had free space.

Dad bought the property from the Finley Estate for $16,000 in 1981. Since Finley would make no repairs, we had little choice but to buy it.

There was a 50' x 100' vacant lot next door. He paid $8.500 for that in 1976. Thus, we had one of the few downtown Palatka parcels with on-site parking. This created assemblage or plottage value where the total is worth more than the sum of the parts.

We had a use for the property and it was affordable. The out of state owner liked us. We knew the neighborhood and did cosmetic repairs, which added value and the rented bay lowered overhead.

Dad's last associate, Jake Jacoway, worked for a convenience store chain and they rented our bay, plus maintained the building for free after 1987.

Parking poaching became a problem which I helped to abate, but never totally solved. Then there was the matter of the buried fuel tank on the back end. We also had a spate of termites which needed treating. Gas space heat was inadequate in cold weather.

In 1985 Dad spent about $7,000 in renovations and modernizations. These included a new roof and central air conditioning. It would be nearly impossible to calculate a rate of return for this property. I sold it in 1993, but had to take a lot in trade for part of the price.

Something's Fishy

The rented half of our duplex office in Palatka was used by a fish store. This was a small family business and they paid $125 month. They complained, but stuck it out four years. They sold the business for $16,000 to Fish Two, who made all sorts of renovations with no lease from us in 1975.

Fish Two was also a family business, but lazier. A year went by and they had a good idea: Carpet in lieu of rent. Dad was a trusting sort, but he also was interested in cash flow. Fish Two dragged out their demise for months by substituting a ceiling fan for rent and an air conditioner for rent.

Fish Two failed to show up one day and eventually Fish One foreclosed on their note. There was nothing of value except aquariums, pumps, feed, etc. This fetched $1,600 or 10 cents on the dollar. This is a typical ratio of value for a business open vs. closed.

The buyer of the contents flushed the gravel from the aquariums down the toilet and Dad got stuck for $200 in plumbing bills. The value of a small business is very hard to determine.

Our fish camp would have been a poor long term business except for one thing---ownership of the riverfront land. Fishing waned as pollution increased. Increasing wealth meant more people had their own boats and equipment. Lawyers on TV urged everyone to sue, driving up insurance rates. Fishing is dangerous for the novice. I saw hooks embedded in ears and bodies turned blood red from too much sun. The land made our camp a good deal over the years.

Buy Land from an Old, Old Friend

Parker Reynolds wanted me to go with him to look at some land for sale in St. Johns County south of Jacksonville. What he really wanted was for me to take half the commission and give him some. This was illegal in 1969, but is legal today. Today the Realtor can share his commission with an unlicensed person who is a party to the transaction.

The land was 120 acres with no road frontage, but there was an access easement. The location at Orangedale was 1/2 mile east of the St. Johns River and about 45 minutes south of

Jacksonville. The heavily wooded tract had a creek running through it. Parker might dam it up to make a lake.

The listing ran out and Parker got to know the owner, an elderly man who lived nearby. Parker wanted to buy this land and retire on it someday. Two years after first contact, Parker got the property. He paid $20,000 or $167 an acre, dirt cheap even then.

Since his purchase the area has grown enormously. General Development put in a project, and the World of Golf is there. Hundreds of small, high class residential projects have occurred in this general area.

One good deal is all you need. Parker was friendly with the seller, familiar with the neighborhood, had a use for the land and it was affordable.

Florida has a tax assessment law known as Greenbelt. As long as your land is classed agricultural, the taxes are low, but if it's classified as residential the taxes soar. The former annual bill might be $1,000, and the latter bill might be $12,000.

In 2006, the land sold to Arvida, developers for $4 million. They owned the land next door and today there is a 4 lane road on site. This 35 year holding period produced a 16% annum return on investment.

Parker died in 1998 at the age of 62 so while he was wise to buy the land, he got nothing out of it but to leave a rich widow.

Buy Many Mismanaged Rental Houses

Ray Vanderslice, my associate, and I were having coffee in 1972 looking for FSBO's (For Sale by Owners). One ad said "Rental house, $1,000 down." I asked Ray to call him. A few days later Ray brought the owner, Rust, by the office. Rust owned 15 block rental houses all over town. Most were in good areas, three bedrooms and in average condition.

Rust's prices and terms were so good I didn't even bother to go inside. I picked out four near my office and bought them with $1,200 down total. I gave Rust second mortgages at 7% payable over 30 years. All the first mortgages were assumable with no qualifying and the second payments ran as low as $18 a month. I carried out one of Roger's dictums, buy below market and get good terms!

Rust and his wife managed these homes, but not very well. Half of the tenants paid no rent or were so far behind they had given up. Two homes required eviction and I hired a painter to fix them up and carry off the trash. That cost another $1,600.

Ten months later, all were full with good paying tenants. I sold all four to one investor. I paid $54,000 and got $62,900 but my return on cash was 250%.

Had I bought all of Rust's homes, I would have bought myself a job. One deal like this can make you a millionaire but managing homes is difficult. Most tenants are okay, but you remember the bad ones. One wag said, "1 don't want to own anything with a bed in it."

Nothing down purchases will cost you double the income. If rent is $400 a month, outgo will be $800 a month. Nothing down is good if you plan to flip the property (sell right away).

Don't Make a Tenant Mad Who Lives Near You

Dad managed lots of cheap property and the files got thick. After his heart surgery in 1988 I threw out thousands of pages. I was friendly toward my tenants, but Dad became friends with his.

Dad owned 1/3 acre in downtown Palatka with the taxi stand in front. In 1959 he added a cottage to its rear, paying $3,500. The paint-less house was rented to Knupp, an immigrant truck driver. It was zoned commercial, so no one minded when he parked his 18-wheeler beside the house. He paid rent of $35/month so the rent multiplier is $3500/$35 = 100 which is a ratio that is fairly consistent throughout the residential rental market and historically valid.

The Knupps were friendly and I liked them. Mother got cancer when I was in high school and during those stressful times, they brought food and cleaned our apartment.

Behind Dad's house was a three-unit apartment he managed for an out of state owner. Florida has a lot of out of state owners. The two-story frame building needed repairs.

A black tenant on social security was accused of rape by a teen girl who hung around the building. As far as we knew, the only thing he was guilty of was drinking. He sat in jail a year before his trial came up. Dad took him his social security check for signature. He kept the apartment, thinking he'd get out any day. Mother got mad about socializing with a black drunk, but Dad didn't care. He was a good judge of character and the man was acquitted.

A white woman in the building quit paying rent. Dad cut off her water. She cut off his water. He cut off her electricity. She egged his car and stole his newspaper. She had a load of fill dirt dumped in Dad's front yard.

The apartment ran down, became vacant, burned and was demolished, as were several others on that street.

Marry a Woman with a House

Martha Osterbrock and I began dating in 1972. She had a small block home on the edge of Jacksonville. It had 1,100 sq. ft. including addition. There was one bath and she had three teenage daughters. We met because of this house. There was a fire in the laundry room and she and her girls lived in the motel which also housed my bar. The home was neat and had a huge lot. The den was added for $1,300. It had attractive ponderosa pine paneling, but the builder forgot to lay down the vapor barrier and the carpet squished. They paid $9,500 for the house in 1956. We married in 1974 and I moved out of my $300 a month apartment and into her $64 a month house. After I got on the VA panel, we fixed the home up with white carpet, remodeled the kitchen, added central heat and air and a 6 foot high wood fence.

Teenage boys lived next door and their house was a mess with cars on blocks. Someone broke into our home and painted slurs on the walls. We were ready to move. The neighborhood had a high percentage of rental houses. The mailman bought up a number of them during the '65 recession. He could tell who was getting the duns and he took them over for back payments.

A government apartment went up next door to the subdivision. Trailers were located to the south. We moved to Holiday Hill, but Martha wanted to keep the old home as an investment and safety net if our marriage bummed.

The first tenant was okay, a topless dancer who paid the rent on time in small bills. Next were two women who looked like men. The air condenser blew up costing $800. When the rent was late I stopped by and smelled the dog odor. Large dogs were inside.

When I got the house back, the damage was enormous. The carpet was ruined and we had to paint the inside. Even the yard had to be repaired.

Martha now knew my advice was right: We should have sold the home right away without renting it. I sold it in 1979 for $26,500 but could have gotten more, sooner and easier by following the above.

Residential Lots Are Tricky Investments

In 1974 I bought a lot down from Martha's Windy Hill house. It was 75' by 200' and I paid $2,500.

I kept getting weed citations from the city. I eventually realized that these citations were the result of a complaint, since the city does not go looking for weeded lots. If you don't mow it, they will and bill you a high price.

Martha's middle daughter, Kelli, was strong and able. I gave her $25 to mow the lot and later found out she hired a sub mower for $15, kept $10 and did nothing.

I sold the lot on contract for deed, but he made no payments so I had to find him and get him to sign a quit claim deed back to me. Another broker sold the lot, but I had to get a zoning variance for a trailer. This shouldn't have been a problem, as trailers were already on this street, but my lot was next to a house that was not well kept. I spoke at the hearing and the woman in the house said she didn't want any trashy trailer next to her. She had been the one ratting on me to the city about weeds. I said her house would shame most trailers. We got the variance; but she threatened to sue me personally. It never happened.

A year after purchase I got $3,500 for the lot, but all the work made it a hollow victory. It closed at the historic Florida Title Building, now demolished. This building had manned elevators and marble finish.

John Rogers said that residential lots are poor investments, but in 1969, I wanted to buy a lot on a canal at Julington Creek, south of Jacksonville for $1,500. Today that lot is worth $200,000, which is a 12.5% return over the 41 year holding period. This time the expert was wrong.

Auction a Victorian Mansion with Contents on the River

In 1975, I was the main appraiser in Palatka. Realtor Paul drove and I followed him to the assignment. We drove down SR 19. He turned down a one-lane rut road and drove another 10 minutes. Huge trees hung over the lane, and it was nearly dark. Suddenly, we burst into the daylight -- and there it was.

Poised on a small hill was a three-story wooden unpainted Victorian mansion. The 100-year-old house had 11,000 sq. ft., a tower and thousands of feet of porches. There were 13 bedrooms but only 2 1/2 baths.

Inside, the plaster was loose and wet. The mansion was completely furnished with antiques, dishes, linens, a cherry wood piano, silver, clothes, everything for proper Victorian living. The home was built as a vacation retreat and was originally accessible only by boat. Amazingly, it had never been vandalized, robbed or burned.

Next to the mansion was the "rec. hall," a three-story wooden building 100' long. It contained a bowling alley/dance floor and six interconnecting bedrooms. There was a guest cottage, dock with boathouse and an added six-car garage. The improvements and tennis court were on six acres of St. Johns River front land.

The property was listed for sale in 1970 for $100,000. Five years went by with no takers. Finally, Realtor Paul offered $85,000 and the estate accepted. Hard-to-get-to property is hard to sell. Paul had $35,000 of his own money, and the rest he was to borrow from a Palatka bank if my appraisal was adequate.

The deal closed and Paul hired an auction company. I didn't think many people would attend this remote offering, but my wife Martha and I went. Cars stacked down the rut road nearly reaching the highway. We walked a mile in sand. The auctioneer worked from a tent between the house and river. Helpers brought out the contents and one-by-one they sold. We bought a dry sink. The auction ran two days with the real estate sold last. The land was sold five different ways with the highest value being the binding sale.

The contents fetched $40,000 and real estate brought $90,000 and Paul kept four of the six acres for himself. Paul earned about $70,000 in 30 days and never picked up a paint brush.

Rent from a Friend Who Is Next Door and in the Same Business

In 1969, Dad suggested I contact Meadows about a job. He owned the post office in Palatka and Dad had some dealings with him and knew him to be wealthy.

The card said 6053 Expressway. What expressway I thought? I didn't know the zip code meant Arlington Expressway, a busy and difficult road with service roads. It connected to the Matthews toll bridge and to downtown. The office had an inverted curved roof that looked like a set of brass knuckles. I dropped in and his secretary led me into the plush confines.

John Meadows was about 65 and a full time real estate investor. He opened up when he realized Dad was my father. He had a Georgia drawl and colorful sayings like "Boy Howdie!" He showed me his list of properties owned, which ran about 30 pages and included gas stations and stores. He didn't want to own houses. He had no job for me. His son Lee was coming into the business. What he did have was a vacancy. I could have a 17' x 30' bay for $75 a month.

Meadows was the second rich real estate man I had met, Rogers being the first. I went back and listened to him some more. He loved to talk, but was so learned I had trouble understanding him. His talk about taxes, stock and politics tended to go over my head.

I studied my office-to-be. There was no ceiling, only the pre-cast concrete curved roof. There was fixed glass in front and back and a back door. At the corners were green fluorescent tubes. Mr. Meadows explained they gave off more lumens! What is a lumen, I wondered. Later I learned he got a good deal on these quirky lights and couldn't pass it up.

The heat pack hung on the rear outside wall. I didn't realize it didn't work until I moved in. This building was really cheap, like the rent. The architecture was never duplicated anywhere else. It had good exposure, though. I moved in February 1970. I used Meadow's copy machine, an old clunker with brown paper you had to peel and separate like Polaroid film.

Lee and I got along well. I did a few sales and appraisals for them, but not the volume I had hoped.

They pumped me for knowledge, too. After a few years I expanded into two bays and paid $250 a month. By this time I had 10 lamps and six portable heaters. By 1980, Lee was in charge and he changed the green tubes for white ones and the light doubled.

During the recession of '81 they lowered my rent. One of many advantages of renting over buying.

Buy a Lake Subdivision

Dad's office was low key. Retired and semi-retired men hung around. Aldrich would come in and sit and exclaim how busy he was and 45 minutes later he was still sitting and still exclaiming how busy he was. He was Dad's first sales associate and a consistent producer. He was short in stature and drove a huge car.

Gunter was big, loud and high energy. He'd come in and ask about lot values. He had bought a lakefront subdivision and sold lots to his friends back in Germany. He charged $5,000 for a 1/3 acre lot, which was double the going rate for a good lake lot in 1972. When he ran out of friends, he ran out of sales.

The project was in South Putnam County near Aldrich's house and branch office of the Cooper Co. Aldrich bought the balance of Gunter's subdivision, about 45 acres for $100,000, nothing down with seller held paper.

Aldrich created more lots out of the back land and gave them lake access. The bulldozer pushed over some aquatic plants, illegal today. Aldrich knew how to price and sell land and in eight years he made a $200,000 profit.

Release clauses called for a master mortgage pay-down of 1.5 times sale price. For every dollar sold, Gunter got $1.50, thus his collateral was protected. Interim bank financing is usually required to fund this type of operation.

You must have cash to wait out the sales process and pay down that mortgage. Many developers fail to realize how long it takes to sell even good land. Also you can get hit with paving or sewer ordinances

Gunter created a two-tier market with non-locals paying double value. This can increase to a three-tier market: Snow birds, locals and repossessions.

Aldrich figured he was paying about $2,222 per acre for the entire project. Lots drawn on paper do not necessarily create value. In other words he could have broken even by reselling as lake land, without selling any lots.

Go to Open Houses

By 1977 Martha and I were ready to move. The Windy Hill house was small, and had only one bathroom. Martha's daughters were ages 12, 14, and 16.

We picked out a neighborhood, Holiday Hill, the same subdivision where Linda and I had lived, but we were looking in the more expensive end. Holiday Hill was well located and well buffered. It's large with an active market so you know what to pay and what to sell for. Values ranged from beginner to luxury.

We rode the area often. We saw an open house with no owner present, just the Realtor, so we went in. The street appeal of Acapulco Rd. was bland, but inside it was great. A den was added with custom bookcases. The hardwood floors gleamed and the required two bathrooms were spacious. The previous owners had made many other improvements, all good quality.

I paid the full list price of $39,000, with $4,000 down and took over the existing mortgage. I got back half the down payment as a split commission. The mortgage was at 9% and Dad said I would go broke.

Martha didn't like some of the cosmetics, but the house was in move-in condition. The only thing wrong was the roof shingles were thick and curled. During the first heavy rain it leaked where the den joined the original house. We had the roof replaced costing $2,300, but it still leaked at the same spot. The front porch leaked, too. Twelve years later we had another roof replacement. All leaking stopped, but this time we paid $3,800.

We have poured money into this house. We have replaced the windows, heat and air, carpet, wallpaper, drapes, remodeled both bathrooms, glassed in the porch, new floor, ceiling fans, added driveway, cut trees, built a pool and garaged the car port.

I like the large lot, 85' x 120'. There is room for Martha's garden, pool, shed, grass and so on. We have good privacy compared to new projects.

The shed was big and ugly. It was off grade, 14' x 16' and built to last. I noticed the light from the bedroom and Martha got up and said, "The shed's on fire." At 2 A.M. I scramble to get my pants on, grab the fire extinguisher and run outside. The fire is beginning to run the wood fences and climb a corner tree. The fire extinguisher is gone in seconds, having no effect. Three fire trucks arrive and put it out.

My neighbor Pionessa removed the shed remains and insurance paid for the tree removal. We were lucky. The cause was probably a cigarette thrown in nearby mulch.

Don't Buy from Crooks

Sid Connor bought St. Johns Riverside Estates in 1975. This sprawling rural subdivision was in Southern Putnam County. It covered 20 sq. miles and had grass roads, if any. The rolling land was used as pasture and did have some paved road frontage on State Road 309.

I met Sid only by phone. He wanted me to do a feasibility study to help him unload the entire property. Meanwhile he was selling lots on a contract for deed to northern buyers. Those buyers were trusting Sid as they had never seen the land. The contract said you get a deed later when you have made all your payments.

Sid would pay half my fee and hire me again. Finally I was appraising lots to keep him out of bankruptcy. I estimated Sid's income from lot sales at $50,000 a month, but he failed to pay his mortgage and the property taxes. He bankrupted the company. I went to the trial, but did not testify. Sid didn't come, but his son did. Hundreds of angry lot buyers filled the courtroom demanding what they had paid for.

Even as the land was taken for unpaid taxes, Sid still sold lots. He was jailed for land fraud. He jumped bail and went to Canada, his home country. He continued to sell lots up there. Bounty hunters found Sid and brought him back to Florida. Then Secretary of State, George Shultz asked that he be given back to his home country, but this was denied and he served a few years in minimum security prison. Sid knew how to dangle bait, but his last letter to me said, sorry things did not work out. And there was no check. It was 1979.

Don't buy on a land contract unless you KNOW the seller is reputable. Don't buy without title insurance. Don't buy without talking to the issuing attorney regarding your title, which is the strength of ownership. Today's Sid land is owned by Putnam County for unpaid real estate taxes, a first lien. What Sid did was the equivalent of passing bad checks.

Land Value

"The Good Earth" is one of Realtors' favorite ad themes. Others are: Under all is the land; they ain't makin no more of it and Buy now before it's all gone! (Where is it going to go)?

When I was with Rogers, we sold 10 acres to Moore Handley, a home improvement store. After a zoning hassle, the sale closed for $75,000. The three piece suited buyer said, "I stole this. I've been paying lots more for sites like this."

The bib-over seller said. "I'da sold this cabbage patch for much less."

After going on my own, Ronnie Clark, a Palatka attorney, hired me to appraise a farm near the interchange of 1-95 and SR 16, the St. Augustine exit. The state had taken a sliver off the parcel and we were going to court. The state said the site was a farm and I said it was a motel site. We won in front of a local jury and today there is a motel on the site. Buy at major Interstate exits.

John bought 400 acres for an office park. This is now Corporate Square. He presold 10 acres to an apartment developer and thus got the down payment for the big parcel. A subsidized complex went in. John sold another 10 acres for the same use.

A few offices went in, but after 10 years and a million dollars of costs, the project sold under duress. This was, among other things, a misjudgment of highest and best use. For every office that was built, 50 homes were built on adjacent land.

I appraised a small lot for the city. I noticed the well, but didn't know it was 3,000 feet deep and 12" wide. It punched into the Florida aquifer and had to be filled under environmental law. Filling the well with concrete cost more than the land was worth.

I appraised 300 acres for a Miami man. He told me he had a standing offer of $10,000 per acre. I asked to see the offer and it read: For all land above the 30' contour line. This worked out to only 155 acres. The remaining land might be seasonally wet and it was near a lake. So, what was $10,000 an acre dropped to $5,166 an acre. This is a classic case of reading the fine print.

In 1985, I appraised 10,000 acres for the Small Business Administration for a $6,000 fee. I hired a plane and flew over the land. After I was finished, I found out there was only one other bid to do the job: $12,000.

During this time I did dozens of farm repossession appraisals for the SBA. (Small Business Administration) Most were in the Live Oak area of Florida. Most showed signs of misspending and mismanagement. There'd be a new roof, but rotten eaves. There'd be a swimming pool, but equipment rusting in the rain. SBA guaranteed loans made by private lenders.

With Rogers, I appraised an acre under the Matthews Bridge. This industrial site was rented for $150 a month. I could find no comparable sales of land under bridges, so I capitalized the rent of $1,800 a year by dividing by 7%, yielding a value of $25,714. The owner had already gotten value for the air rights he gave up when the bridge was built. Under fee simple ownership, you own up to the edge of the sky and to the center of the earth.

In Putnam County, I appraised land subject to pollution from the coal-fired Seminole Electric plant. While pollution was evident, I could find no value loss. Likewise people buy near power lines even though there has been talk of cancer and even though high winds could fell a charged line onto the house.

Developers get into financial trouble waiting for sales. Few developers can stand the sometimes near-interminable wait for the buyer. The best site can take years to sell. Paying cash is the only safe way to hold land. Paying cash is also a powerful downward bargainer of the price.

In Florida you need to keep the Greenbelt assessment category available to farmers. Sometimes, developers will plant a few trees or vegetables to qualify.

Options

When Hillary Clinton made $100,000 on a $1,000 investment in grain futures that was close to an option in real estate. It is a one-way contract favoring the buyer. The option holder can back out, but not the seller. This high leverage tool gives the user time to develop, finance, assemble, pre-sell or resell.

Leslie optioned 10 acres. He paid $1,000 for the right to pay $100,000 one year later. During this one year, he pre-sold two one-acre tracts for $50,000 each. Of course, full disclosure is needed so buyers aren't deceived. Leslie takes minimal money to closing and gets a free eight acres.

Disney operatives used the option to assemble 28,000 acres south of Orlando, Florida. In 1965 land was acquired for an average of $180/acre or $5 million. In 2004, they have 30,500 acres, 75% of which is still vacant. (*Some Kind of Paradise*, Mark Derr.)

Owners being assembled often want to get the same money as the other people are getting, regardless of price or value.

Options to purchase the real estate are sometimes given in business leases. Even if the business fails, the option has value if the real estate increased in value. The option can be used on any type of real estate, not just land.

Oil drillers or miners can option large tracts while they hunt for their treasure.

An option is a form of contract. A contract is an agreement between two or more people usually to perform some work in exchange for money. In order for a contract to be enforceable, it must be legal, should be in writing and have consideration or money involved. The parties must be sane and sober. Minors (under age people) are not competent to make contracts.

Some investors never use a purchase and sale agreement, but always an option agreement. This limits buyer liability if the purchase fails to close. If the option holder fails to close on the transaction, he loses the money paid for the option. If he closes, the option money may apply toward the purchase price. The word "option" should appear on the document. Always disclose material facts.

The option is the "flipper's" friend. In an inflating market you can control the property for few months without ever taking title and incurring those expenses and risk. Just be sure your seller knows you are not taking title. Flipping may be done by assigning (selling) the purchase contract.

Auctions

Auctions are often used to sell foreclosures. A 19-story building in Jacksonville cost $15 million to build in 1962. It was sold at auction in 1978 for $3.6 million. The sale took two minutes and there was only one bidder, the mortgagee (lender).

Auctions are used for single-family homes. They can be held online or by mail. An auction can guarantee results. Auctions can be national or international, so a good, accurate and honest description is necessary. Appraisals are an integral part of the auction process.

Don't be late for an auction, as the first units are often sold absolute, that is, regardless of price. Also, stay late, as the last units may be sold absolute to close out the project.

Auctions create interest, which creates value. People will even buy a sealed box as when mini-warehouse contents are auctioned off. They are buying excitement and the unknown.

Auctioneers are skilled at generating excitement. Entertainment also helps. A land auction had a performer blow himself up. Contests will try to get your name and address for future auctions. Shills, or fake bidders, may drive up prices.

Auctions create markets on the spot. No one knows exactly what will happen when an auction begins. Real estate that otherwise could take years to sell, can be moved during the excitement of an auction in just a few hours. It is hoped that friends of bidders will join in the competitiveness.

The raffle method gives the property to the lucky winner, but a ticket can cost $1,000 or more and income tax is due, if you win.

The federal government is authorized to auction or sell the properties of convicted drug dealers. They do a good business in south Florida.

Internet auctions and eBay offer collectibles and properties. eBay is a potent force in auctioning properties, especially for famous or infamous sellers.

Lease auctions are held. Koger Center on Jacksonville's Beach Blvd. was offered absolute for part of 150,000 sq. ft.

Read *Hidden Treasures* by Leslie and Leigh Keno for memorable auctions of furniture held at Christie's and Sotheby's. An American table brought $8 million.

Surveys

A survey is an engineering drawing of your property. It shows land corners, buildings, physical and legal characteristics.

They are expensive and all lenders require them. They are also necessary to obtain title insurance.

During college I worked as part of a survey crew for Hudson Pulp and Paper Co. in Palatka, now Georgia Pacific. I was a hacker. I helped clear sighting lines using a machete. Every night I soaked in a tub of soda water to relieve insect bites.

You need a survey even if there is no lender. A lakefront cabin buyer was dismayed when the neighbor fenced off his road. A survey might have warned this buyer.

Rogers bought 130 acres to be bisected by Interstate 95 in 1960. He ended up filing a suit to quiet title as there was a 30-acre difference between his survey and the state's. Back then he thought the valuable land fronted on the interstate and they sold the interchange parcels cheaply. They lost in condemnation court as access to the two halves was damaged and not paid for adequately by the state.

The surveyor writes the legal description without which the title (ownership) cannot pass (be sold). Most houses have a lot and block, but land can have metes and bounds (angles and directions) taking a full page to write.

A common problem found by surveys is encroachments. A neighbor's fence is actually a few feet over on your land. His eave projects over your land. A trail or cut through at some point becomes a legal road. An encroachment is a flaw on the title, a dent in your ownership. Establishing land area is most important. Land will sell over and over again. Parties believe it is 10 acres, but finally the land gets valuable enough to be surveyed and it is eight acres.

Elevations can be established so you will know how much high ground there is. Trees can be located so you know where to place buildings and save the most trees. Drainage patterns are discovered. Wells and septic tanks can be located. The flood zone is named.

Surveys outdate. Roads are widened and buildings built or torn down. Pieces are sold off. Laws change. The surveyor is registered with the state and he has a license number and seal. His name and address must appear on the drawings.

The tax assessor or property appraiser has ownership maps which have some survey characteristics and they are available at a nominal price. Check there first.

Title

Title is your strength of ownership. The most complete estate is the fee simple estate. This is what most of us own. If you mortgage your property, the estate is weakened by the claim of the mortgagee (mortgagee = lender; mortgagor = borrower). If you rent your property, the claim is weakened by the claim of the tenant (owner = leasor; tenant = leasee).

The strongest estate would be the paid off un-leased fee simple estate. It has value because you can use it, rent it, give it away, sell all or part of it, and build on it.

All estates are subject to real estate taxes and zoning laws. A few areas have health and safety codes in lieu of zoning.

Mineral rights can be conveyed or retained. You can sell your land and keep mineral rights. Be sure to provide for the right to drill or otherwise extract the minerals.

Air rights mean you own to the limit of the atmosphere above your land, subject to aircraft.

Title insurance companies protect your ownership against unknown claims. A title search is done before the policy is issued. The public records at the courthouse are examined. Known defects are not covered or are excepted from the policy.

Attorneys will require the title to be made whole if the chain of title is broken. This may be cured by signatures or affidavits. An ex-wife may have to sign away any interest or a will found and recorded.

The most common title flaws include unpaid real estate taxes and women who get married, changing their name. Most title flaws are minor and easily corrected.

One may obtain an abstract in lieu of title insurance. This is a paper trail of past ownerships and claims-sort of a family tree for land. Dad would do this to save money.

Joint ownerships include Tenancy by the Entireties, usually a husband and wife. When one dies, that share automatically passes to the other owner.

Other tenancies allow a deceased's share to pass to heirs, so you can end up owning with a stranger. Corporations and partnerships can own property. An attorney experienced in real estate is required for your investment success.

Title to land can be acquired through war, force or violence. Treaties and purchase agreements also forged title in the early days of our country.

Countries bordering the Arctic Circle are claiming land under the ice and water. In 2007 Russia planted a flag on this property. Canada, Denmark and Norway also want resources at the North Pole.

The moon will become a hotbed of ownership disputes as technology allows the mining of its minerals.

In recent years, many millions of dollars, gifts and grants have been given to Indians to set old wrongs right.

The prime title dispute today is between the Israelis and Palestinians. Another big problem was when Fidel Castro's Cuba took property from U.S. firms in 1960.

On the individual level, squatters have rights. If they live there long enough and pay taxes on the land, they own it.

Title insurance companies pay only 5% of premiums out in claims, but title insurance is still a necessity because you could lose the entire property. Sellers who don't own the property are a big crime problem.

Fences

"Good fences make good neighbors," Robert Frost (American poet, 1874-1963) said. A fence should run just inside your property line. A survey is recommended for accurate fence placement.

Fences are usually wire or wood. Wire is often chain-link and wood should be pressure-treated, cedar or cypress. The picket fence is wood with a see-through design. Wire is see-through, unless you put Venetian blinds in it. Vinyl fences are bright white and usually ring projects, but are now being seen around individual houses. They don't rot.

A fence will shrink a yard. A six-foot privacy fence makes a yard seem much smaller. Shorter or see-through fences have less impact. Some people use cross fencing for dog runs or pools.

It is important to contain animals within fences. Some thoughtful owners put down metal flashing to stop pets from digging underneath, and electric wires also stop animal aggression.

A fence can give your property personality and be useful, too. Dad had a wire fence along the sidewalk and vines grew through it.

Most jurisdictions require a pool yard to be fenced for safety, plus, if you have small children, the pool itself can be fenced. Attractive styles are available.

A fence can lower value. You can't control people's taste. Graffiti artists can also strike. Fred painted his house purple with fence to match. A wood fence will burn rapidly and can bring fire right up to your house.

Some say retention ponds or lakes should be fenced for safety, like a swimming pool, and others say they hurt the water view.

Fences can guide community development. Gates are used to announce a subdivision entrance or town entrance. Some subdivisions prohibit fences. This makes a nice open project, but pets suffer.

Fences can block streets and divert traffic, as with 1st Street in Neptune Beach. Car racing is stopped, too.

Fencing was placed down the center of an expressway to cut down on people running across the highway. It kept a skidding car from crossing into oncoming traffic, but hurt business.

Fences have been used by countries to keep invaders out (the Great Wall of China) and to keep dissidents in (the Berlin Wall). A moat around a castle is an inverted fence.

Federal authorities discovered 12 tunnels under the fence along the U.S.-Mexico border since Sept. 11, 2001. A fence is being used to separate fighting Palestinians and Israelis.

By 1818 the "people's house," the White House, had too many people visiting it and an iron fence was installed around its perimeter. They began locking it when a vagrant was found inside sleeping.

Celebrities like high fences for protection from zealous fans and paparazzi (photojournalists). Zoning regulates fence height in some areas, but in South Florida hedges can be as high as an elephant's eye.

Fences are placed on beaches to resist erosion and to build up sand blown by prevailing wind. Sea oats can serve this purpose, too.

Life Estate Can Boost Value

Mom and Dad (not mine) owned 20 acres on the edge of Palatka. They built their cottage 45 years ago. As time passed the town grew out to them and the road was four-laned. Dad passed away, but Mom stayed and gardened. Her house was at one end of the 20 acres. The acreage had 1,320' on the highway and 660' of depth. All the land was in random pasture except one acre where her house was.

Shopping center people approached Mom, but she was happy there and money was not needed. When she wasn't gardening or doing house work, she watched a black and white TV.

Broker Bob took the time to get to know Mom. He convinced her to have the land appraised. It was valued at $200,000. Mom exclaimed, "It can't be worth that much. Why I'd sell to that church across the street for $100,000 when I get old." She was already 82.

Bob explained that the church had no money, but the shopping center developer had $200,000 and she could keep the 10 acres nearest her house. A tree row was planted down the middle as buffer. Mom sold, but retained a life estate of 10 acres where she lived.

Mom can stay in her house for as long as she lives. Upon her death the shopping center is vested with title on the full 20 acres and maybe by then will want to expand. Mom made a donation to the church and bought a color TV. Every day she gardens.

Bob was patient and knew deals are personal and not always driven by money. He got a commission and the town got a larger tax base. By taking the time to get to know the seller and her needs, he enriched all concerned.

Buy Riverfront Corporate Surplus

During World War II, Glop, a mining company, was active in Duval County. They stripped the land and left deep piles of white sand. Some of this land has now been reclaimed.

Glop built two riverfront homes in Mandarin south of downtown Jacksonville for executives. One sat on five acres on the St. Johns River.

Glop left Jacksonville in 1960 and listed the big house at $100,000. The price was fair, but there were no buyers. Glop was an indifferent owner who would not notice the existence or absence of this property from their balance sheet. Seven years later it was still listed, with Fudd. The Hicks loved it, but only had $45,000. Fudd said let's make the offer. Glop accepted without fanfare, and was glad to be rid of the headache.

The Buckmann Bridge was completed. This is part of the 1-295 Beltway. Mandarin was opened up to Orange Park and values boomed. The local rich and famous bought in this area as did the social climbers and wannabes. Prestige makes buyers crazy. River front land is a good investment because of its limited supply.

Hicks died in 1985 and I appraised the estate for $450,000. The return was 12.9% per annum over the 18 year holding period. Hicks got rich and had fun doing it. One good buy is all you need.

Fudd was a very patient broker. He was also courageous to make such a low offer. Some sellers get mad over low offers and the listing is blown, but after seven years Fudd figured, what the hell! Hicks made their money when they bought. It pays to think poor.

The IRS and Donation

I appraised a large tract of river swamp for a wealthy Palatka client. There was some high ground and some peat or other minerals plus a lot of river frontage. My report was $2,000 per acre resulting in a huge write-off under donation rules at the time. The next year we got more aggressive and my value went up to $3,000 an acre. The accountant should have caught it, but didn't. The difference in values triggered the audit. I did not show proper respect for IRS auditors who had appraised the same land at $100 acre. I said, "See you in court."

A little known rule, passed in 1984, allowed them to take $4,000 from me for "aiding and abetting" a taxpayer in filing a fraudulent return. No trial, no hearing, just guilty. The client ditched me and I was unable to find an attorney willing to take this case.

We had better luck with a proposed cemetery. This client owned land next to a real cemetery and he drew lots on his map. A plot sold for $300 for a 3' x 10' parcel. This is $10 a sq. ft. or $435,600 per acre; a tremendous sum of money for Putnam County. The donation got the client audited, but I was not bothered.

Another client had acquired land by tax deed for only $150 an acre. After waiting a few years, the title was perfected. The appraisal was for $1,500 an acre, which made a great donation and write-off for him.

I donated a small lot in Palatka to the Baptist Church. This went well and is a later chapter.

Trade Land for Debt Relief

In 1981 I appraised several land parcels in Flagler County, home of Palm Coast. Glenn Stephens was a Palatka accountant who got me many jobs. This one was an estate with little cash. My fee was $1,500 of which $1,000 was paid in land and $500 in cash. The land was 50' x 50' approximately, but it fronted on the Atlantic Ocean. It was at the corner of SR A1A and 12th St. North in the City of Flagler Beach. It had tight vegetation cover, but no building permit was available. They wouldn't even let me put up a for sale sign.

The tax assessment was $900 and the taxes were $15 a year. I had a lot of fun with this lot and it generated good conversation. I made up a mailer priced at $20,000. They built wooden stairs in the street end beside the lot.

Palm Coast is an ITT project and has attracted many a northern retiree. It made Flagler County one of the fastest growing counties in Florida. The area is north of Daytona Beach,

You could build on the lot if regulations permitted. Plenty of lots like this in California have houses on them. A few of these lots were built on before the set back line was established. Picnic tables are in the road right of way.

By 1991, I was suffering from the extensive recession of that time. By 1993, I was dealing with the Chevy Chase credit card collection agency. I owed them $8,000 and traded the lot for the debt relief.

The $7,000 gain was taxable as income even though there was no cash involved. The "sale" represents a return of 17.55% per annum over the 12-year holding period.

The IRS is always your partner in real estate. Other trades I benefited from include an office sign for an appraisal of his sign store and office security for an appraisal of some commercial property at Jacksonville Beach.

Get a Will and Keep It Simple

In 1982, I appraised 300 acres which were inherited by six children. There was no will, so under Florida law each child inherited 1/6 of all the land. My job was to appraise out six equally valued parcels. Shared ownership is almost impossible to sell except to other share owners. The rolling land had timber, pasture, creeks, oak hammocks, muck, swamp, a power line easement, road frontage, and other differences. I did the best I could to appraise six equally valued parcels.

Fortunately, all six children were grown adults, or a guardian would have had to be appointed, taking more time and money. The heirs sold their parcel, lived on it, or did whatever they wanted with their recently created, fee simple plots.

In 1974, Stevens died. I went to the courthouse and for a small fee got copies of his will from the probate office. He left by will his 35 acre plot on the river to two heirs. One half went to a museum and one half went to a school. Stevens had relatives, but no children. The conveyance was restricted in that if either heir used the land for anything except woods, the relatives would inherit instead.

This restriction ran for 30 years so after 2004, the land was used by the Episcopal High School for their track and field events. The school bought the other half from the museum. This land is across the street by my Atlantic Blvd. office.

If you have any assets at all, you need a will.

Escheat is the power of the state to take property owned by person who dies with no heirs and no will. (*Real Estate for the New Practitioner* by Clayton Curtis).

Don't Buy a Fish Camp Next to a Man with 50 Cats

The St. Johns River flows north through Palatka, Jacksonville and empties into the Atlantic Ocean at Mayport, Florida.

Our fish camp had a high bank held in place by oaks and bushes. Once I remember a tree falling and taking part of the bank with it. The river was tidal and changed level about a foot. It flowed noticeably and could get very rough.

Wooden steps went down to the dock. There was always an odor of fish or bugs. Speaking of odor, one time a dead alligator of at least 16' floated in and stopped. Dad and I pushed it with oars down to our neighbor's place.

I loved being on the river. It was so quiet you could hear people talking a mile away, if the breeze was right. Mist or fog rising off the water was better than church.

Duck hunters competed with fishermen for usage. One time Dad and I heard a blast and then shotgun pellets fell all around us. The hunter was out of sight around a bend.

Panther could be seen across the river, which was part of the Ocala National Forest. Snakes could drop into your boat if you were near the shore, but they could not get in the boat if swimming in the water.

Another boy and I put on waders and started down the bank. Part of the river had a beach and part was swamp. I saw a snake drop into the water in front of me and in back of him. He didn't believe me at first, but then panic set in and we walked back on land.

Blind mosquitoes would swarm in the spring and fall. They would die by the millions into snowdrift-like banks, making a huge stink.

Hyacinths became the scourge of the river. This floating plant completely blocked the river at times. Small boats couldn't move through the morass.

Our terrier was brought with us from Pittsburgh and thought the hyacinth throng was solid land. It jumped off the dock and got the surprise of its life. It blamed the dock and never went near it again.

I did not know how to swim. This was dangerous being at a fish camp. The river was too dirty to swim in anyway. Near Welaka to the south, was a spring of clear, cold water. Water flowed out of a deep hole in the center. Dad tried to teach me to swim here, but nothing worked until I got in college.

The fish camp land dipped down into a creek at the south line. Across the creek was another great riverfront tract of about six acres; vacant except for a paint-less shack. Large oaks hid the shack from view until you got right up on it.

Charles Heath was about 65 and he lived in that shack. He never bathed and he made his own wine from puff balls or berries that grew wild. He was harmless except when he got drunk and stripped naked and passed out in front of our cabins.

Charlie owned about 50 cats that swarmed over our customers cleaning fish. I made a bow and arrow and shot at them, but never knew if I hit them or not. Usually, the arrow was lost in the dense woods and underbrush.

Dad got me a BB rifle and said, "Keep the cats out of here." I accepted the mission. Today I wince at the cruelty, but this was war and I was the general.

Charlie would bum rides from us into town. By this time our '48 Olds was torn and dented. Dad used the luxury car as a truck. With all windows down, Charlie still stunk so bad we all gagged.

I'd sneak over and peer inside his cabin. I never saw him in it and I don't think he ever saw me. He did start giving away cats. We thought he'd die in there, but I never knew what happened to him.

We worried that Charlie would start a fire, either accidentally or on purpose. There was no defense if a fire got out of control. The next owner of our camp set traps for the cats and threw them into the river.

Sell Before the Plant Closes

In 1976, Dad bought a vacant corner lot for $1,500 from an elderly widow who lived out of state. It was in the same block as our Palatka office and faced the back street.

Dad gave the lot to me. Pennyman, who was a good client of Dad's, bought the lot from me for $3,000 cash. Pennyman's wife died and his plans for Palatka real estate changed. He left town and I bought the lot back from him.

In 1983, I gave Pennyman $4,000 for the lot, but with only $500 down and the balance seller held at $46 a month. I was always a sucker for a low down payment. I thought it possible that if our office grew, we might need this lot for parking.

The other back corner of this block was occupied by the Coca Cola Bottling Company. I used to watch the bottles being filled as a boy. Their large two-story brick building was built in 1911 and is architecturally significant. Since that time, they added a metal building.

In 1985 Coca Cola asked me what I'd sell the lot for. I said $10,000. They said that was ridiculous. They had an appraisal in file that would not justify that kind of money.

The lot was 50' x 100' and on the open market would be worth about $5,000. It was zoned commercial, but was off the main street, St. Johns Ave. It was across from a school and you could build a house on it.

Sixty days later, Coke said they would pay the $10,000 and had to close right away. Who knows what stresses were being felt inside their organization? They had found an appraisal for $10,000 and my return was 47% per annum.

They cut down my pecan tree, paved the lot and fenced it. Then they parked trucks on it. In 1990, Coke closed the entire facility and left Palatka.

I owned this lot twice, doubling our money the first time and doubling plus half the second time.

Timing is crucial, and buy next to someone who will need you. Good as this deal was, the lot beside it sucked.

Buy a House, Convert It to an Office, but Don't Take Out the Kitchen

I found 6544 Atlantic Blvd. in the multiple listing. It was a vacant brick house of 980 sq. ft., plus porches and garage. The asking price was $52,500 in 1981. It had been a rental. It was built in 1949 and had hardwood floors and plastered walls.

The lot was great at 75' x 175' and beside a busy corner and Regions Bank. The house was set well back and trees cut the traffic noise way down. Aiding access was a traffic light and center turn lane.

The property was paid for, so there was no mortgage to get in the way. I paid $49,000 with only $2,500 down and the balance seller held at 12% and $600 a month. I wanted it paid for in 12 years. There were no points, appraisal and I doubt if there was even a credit check.

At closing, the young attorney advised me of deed restrictions. I knew zoning was okay and didn't I think about deed restrictions since the bank was there. I kept a low profile and by 1999 they had expired.

The minute I lit my sign, a zoning violation was slipped through the door. The bank got around that, too. Ratting neighbors enforce most zoning violations.

We fixed the house up and Kelli and Steve Denton did much of the work. Martha's daughter was also helpful cleaning my rental houses, which came later.

Naturally I banked next door. A robber with a shotgun drove through the drive-in window lane. The girls locked the door and called 911. The police took this idiot away. I began to get robbed, too, but only after I'd gone home. They took cokes, beer, a radio, my check writer and so on. I beefed up security, but still got hit.

One day right after a break-in a casual man dropped by selling security systems. He had monitored the police radio and knew I'd been hit. I could get a complete system for $900 which I didn't have. He would not take 90-day terms. Later I drove by his address and nothing was there.

Don't buy security the day after the break-in. Soon I looked up an established company in the phone book and had a complete security system installed.

In 1992, the bank built a new building and tore down the old one. Their driveway comes within two feet of my line.

An old guy in an old car got the accelerator and brake mixed up and slammed into a tree, which kept my building from serious harm. After that, the bank installed posts guarding my property.

Busy suburban streets are good investments because zoning and traffic patterns limit the supply of good sites. The new bank has high powered lights, lessening crime.

When I bought the office, Dad made the first payment for me saying he wouldn't be around to make the last one.

Not only was Dad around, but Uncle Conrad's estate made the last 28 payments for me.

In 2008, I left Atlantic Blvd. and built an office in my back yard. The 15' by 25' building has a wall air unit and full bathroom with shower. It cost $45,000 which I got on a home improvement loan at an unbeatable low rate with Region's Bank.

The recession allowed me to get a low interest rate and quick construction. The place was essentially built by one man who only rarely had a helper.

The old office is now on its fourth Realtor. I keep dropping the price, but to no avail. We took out the kitchen in 1981 when we bought it, but now wish I had it back. During a recession, commercial zoning may not be worth anymore than residential.

In 2010, I replaced the heat and air, but the backyard air condenser was stolen a week later.   Sam Folds had it on TV, the real estate channel.

The insurance lapsed after 30 days and insuring a vacant building is prohibitive.   Once I moved out, the property became a problem.   New handicap laws may hamper business usage of it.

Sell to Rich People When They Want to Buy

Burger City decides to expand. They want to add 200 outlets per year for the next three years. They will option several sites per town or neighborhood and then close on the best one. Their operatives can be young, right out of college and the identity of the buyer is not disclosed.

Speed of acquisition is much more important than the cost of a site. Burger places gross millions of dollars per year, so it doesn't matter much if a site costs $300,000 or $600,000. Also, they tend to pay the same regardless of the size of the town. The president or officer in charge will be pleased if the target number of sites is met. Cost is secondary.

Sell to this buyer. You may never do better. Buy near this buyer. Burger places tend to cluster and if McDonalds buys, Burger King is sure to follow. Some streets lay dormant for years and then everybody buys: banks, restaurants, shopping centers, etc. Commercial land values can remain unchanged for a decade and then triple overnight.

Corporations often don't think about their real estate needs until they are desperate. The real estate man is often a secretary. Realty files are buried in dusty closets. They won't ask you what you want for your lot until they have to expand. You can charge about double value at this point. It could cost them millions of dollars to move.

Don't get greedy. Donald Trump built a casino around a house in Atlantic City. Once they move on or solve the problem your value can dive.

Buy Before the Road Is Built

Eloise and her architect husband were diving and water enthusiasts. They wanted a waterfront home, but didn't have the money.

Ahop, a beaches developer, optioned 10 acres on one of the tributaries connecting with the Intra-Coastal Waterway and the Atlantic Ocean.

There was no road, but he accessed it by boat and got copies of the tax assessor's maps which acted as a crude survey. He drew a proposed subdivision including 15 waterfront lots.

In 1980, he sold six waterfront lots for only $10,000 each. Eloise and family bought one. The road was to be built in one year and their lot would be worth $30,000.

Ahop bought the 10 acres with the presale money and borrowed enough to build the roads and do the engineering. He sold out in four years, making $250,000 net clear.

Eloise's lot was smaller than they thought it would be. This is just one of the many risks of preconstruction buying. Ahop paid the closing costs to compensate them.

Good deed restrictions were recorded and the one street subdivision developed with high quality homes.

Buy inaccessible waterfront from a developer you trust.

Eloise got her dream house, a three-story custom designed edifice. Of course, flood insurance was necessary.

Cheap Rental House Poor Investment

San Jose Village should have been nice. It was attractively laid out and well located. There were four one-story units per building with contemporary saw tooth roofs.

It was built of T-111, factory wood siding and cars parked in the open. There were no trash bins and no maintenance fees.

In 1984, I bought a unit for $32,000, considerably under the market at the time. They were trading for $39,000, but the young couple wanted to leave town and I gave them $5,000 in cash and took over the FHA mortgage.

My unit was 900 sq. ft., two bedrooms, one bath with central heat and air, laundry room, vaulted ceiling and pull down stairs. There were kitchen appliances.

My first tenant, a recovering drug addict, was my best tenant. The rent was $300 to $350 per month. A girl tenant complained about the air conditioning, but when I inspected the unit, the sliding glass door was open.

During the boom years of 1985 to 1987 I hired a management company. This was a disaster. They let the unit sit vacant for months and it seemed all the repairmen were relatives.

The project was built cheaply and units began to run down. Metal additions appeared along with pink paint. Repossessions were marked by high weeds and non-drive cars, some on blocks.

After the '87 stock crash I had little to do, so I took back the management. The saw-tooth roof design guaranteed leaking and was un-fixable.

Rummy, a car salesman, moved in. He wanted to paint in lieu of rent and I said okay. He wanted to put in a bar and I said okay.

One Saturday when the rent was late I drove down early and knocked on the door. No one answered, but the door drifted inward. I saw the white morass spilling over the kitchen counter (the bar) when the pit bull attacked. I could smell dog as I ran for my car.

I started blowing the horn and a man I'd never met came out with another dog, a huge black animal. Rum had painted all right, but not behind the bushes. I evicted Rum and whoever else lived there.

My last tenant was a pregnant, unemployed waitress living in a sea of cigarette butts. I told her she would have to leave.

I sold the unit for the mortgage balance of $27,000 in 1991. A year later that buyer let it repossess. Values reached a low point of $15,000.

Before the tax law of '86 severely limited write offs, some investors bought entire buildings, or four units at a time. The value of these units in 2011 was $33,000.

Look in the Daylight

Look at night, but don't buy until you see it during the day. Look at it several times. Take a flashlight for dark corners or power off situations. Have the water and electric turned on before buying. Check for bulb dimming and plumbing hissing and banging.

Open all doors and windows. If they won't open, settlement may be the cause. One guy put toilets in all his closets. Watch for door hell, i.e. doors hitting one another. Metal bi-fold closet doors can sound like squeaky thunder.

Take all paintings off the walls. One divorce house I appraised had bullet holes. Lift all rugs. One house had hardwood around the edge and plywood in the center, under the rug.

Nudge the toilets. If they are loose the floor underneath may be rotten. Put a marble on the floor and see if it rolls. If it does, settlement may mean foundation failure. Look in vanities for plumbing leaks. Gently press down the floor of the vanity and kitchen sink cabinets with your foot.

Don't buy a pier house unless you plan to skirt the air space. Fire insurance won't cover a pier house because they bum like a rocket. Insurance may not pay if additions were done without a building permit.

Get a termite report before you close the deal. You can also make the purchase contingent upon proper condition as shown by a professional inspector. FHA and VA appraisals also inspect for repairs.

Roof shingles should lie flat. If they are thick and curled there could be failure. Spots on the ceiling are usually a sign of leaking or duct moisture. New shingles in a sea of old shingles means patching. If it leaked once, it either still does or soon will.

Cut bushes away from the house and cut trees away from the eve. Trees leaning on a roof are a highway for termites and a hammer for wind damage.

Carry a pocket knife and stick it into dark spots on the wood siding. It may push right in, meaning the wood is totally rotten.

Look under the house if off grade, and in the attic. Carry a flash camera and use it in dark spots. You will be amazed at the detail it will pick up.

If you see a problem, there are many more you don't see. Don't buy if the building needs major repairs.

Don't criticize the house in front of the seller, but do ask him questions. You can usually tell if he is lying. You can make your purchase contingent upon the seller doing certain repairs, but you cannot make him do a good job.

Make a list of deficiencies and have a contractor give you a bid to fix the items before buying. Regarding the seller's statements, believe but verify.

A skilled buyer can criticize the fool out of a property and still have the seller like him. Lay off blame on a third party. "I like the wallpaper all right, but it'll make my wife puke."

Not always possible, but look during the rain. You will see any roof leaks and also yard drainage problems.

Hire a home inspector. Some buyers hire 2 home inspectors. Don't have them come at the same time.

Buy Low, Sell High

Rogers owned a lot of property. He inherited much of it and let it rot. In 1968 John "gave" Earl and me a small block house for the mortgage balance of $6,000. Our contribution was to fix the place up and sell it and we'd divide the profit three ways.

Earl did most of the physical work and I headed up the sales efforts. I put the house in multiple listing. Another broker brought us a full price contract at $9,500 VA. One day after we signed the VA deal, a buyer walked in with a full price cash offer which we had to turn down. The cash deal would have netted us more money sooner. The VA buyer took over six months to qualify.

After starting my own office, Meadows and my salesman and I bought a small block house for $6,000. We fixed it up and sold it FHA for $9,000. The only trouble was the FHA appraisal came in at $7,500. I was in the middle of my divorce and signed the deal. We lost $500 at closing and I had to fix a leaking roof.

Despite these ventures, today's center of profit is still buy low, sell high. Investors are active in purchasing homes foreclosed on by lenders. They pay half of retail, fix them up and resell. They have fix-up crews and do a volume business.

Guards watch over the appliances, as they can be stolen. Equipment is often installed the day of closing. Carpet is stolen. Spot lights are used and watchful neighbors enlisted.

Some buyers are credit impaired. They are damaged by car repossessions, divorces or layoffs. Some investors take credit impaired buyers by using a seller-held mortgage, contract for deed or rent-to-own agreement. The price or interest rate is then jacked up above retail.

Other sources of cheap buys are divorces and financially distressed owners. Investors comb the sale by owner section of the newspapers and place ads "We buy houses, any condition. Fast cash, don't ruin your credit".

The "fixer upper" has been a boon to some neighborhoods. The market is livelier and more upwardly mobile. It's better to have some market than none at all.

Buy the transfer. The person who has been transferred out of town for his job may be served by a company which buys the house. These companies may pressure the appraiser to be conservative so the place will move. Often pools and other expensive features are given away.

Also, sell to a transferred person. This person lives in a motel with children and needs to buy quickly. If they like your place, they will not quibble over the asking price.

The short sale has become a market saving institution. It's pre-foreclosure and most are in good shape. The bank eats the loss and most losses are paid for by the tax-payers. It makes it easier to walk away from a too high mortgage obligation and makes the mortgage more similar to a lease.

Dealing with Appraisers

Rules are somewhat the same as for dealing with brokers and salesmen. Turn on all the lights, unlock all doors and put away pets.

Tell the appraiser what he needs to know, but don't follow him around talking. The best way is to write a summary of salient facts about the house, such as when the roof or heat was replaced, and give it to him.

It's all right to give comparable sales. He might not have the crucial one. Give a survey if you have one, but be sure he measures the house anyway. Surveys can distort square foot computations.

Tell the appraiser what you want. He can't read your mind. There are two kinds of clients, those who want to know what it's worth and those that want to make a deal happen.

Be nice to everyone. You never know who your appraiser is going to be. A cop let me out of a ticket because I had done him some small favor on an appraisal five years earlier.

If your appraisal comes in low, examine it carefully. Find the comparable sale which indicates the lowest value for your house after adjustments; the bottom line. Submit another sale to take its place.

Check the facts, such as square footage, age, number of rooms, heat, air, and check the math. It's all simple math, but you might need the help of another appraiser or Realtor.

What constitutes living area is a big point of controversy. Enclosed porches are often a judgment call and sometimes a little vinyl flooring or new air duct will boost value.

Check basics. Did he give you credit for a double garage or fireplace? Overlooking the obvious is a common flaw.

Appraising is both an art and a science. People make value by their actions in the market place. An appraisal is written by someone of experience and backed up by facts. If there are two signatures on your report, a "leg man" probably did the field work and extra care is needed in checking the report.

Have the sense to call an appraiser. An old guy thundered about my $300 fee, "I won't pay it." He sold his house on a commercial acre for half its market value.

It's a tired phrase that the 3 most important factors in real estate are location, location and location. Gradually, as I learned appraisal, it turned out the three most important factors are location, square footage of living area and condition.

Appraisal considerations are: What is the fee? How long will it take? How qualified is he or she?

Buy a House with the Pool Already There

In 1985, Martha decided to put in a back yard pool. Pool building is major construction involving all aspects of the trade and pool shysters are common. We paid $15,000 and placed a second mortgage on Acapulco Rd.

The drainage of the lot changed and the yard was in shock for six months. The power company can close your pool if they deem lines are too close. This can happen after you get permitted from the city.

Six years later we had to have the pool re-Marcited. Marcite is the smooth plaster-like concrete that goes on the inside and prevents leaking. It looks like cake frosting when being applied. That cost $2,500 and 6 years after that we spent $3,500 for another Marcite job. Proper cleaning reduces the wear on the Marcite.

We didn't get a dive board which requires 8 feet of depth. So our six feet of depth results in more play area and is better for smaller children. We got a vacuum which roams around sucking up small debris that falls in the pool. Our dog thought the Polaris was alive and stalked it.

There is an underwater light for night swimming. The reflections off the water make interesting light patterns on our home and in the trees. We have a pool maintenance person who cleans it and keeps the pumps running. Rental homes with pools are discouraged.

As an investment, a pool is like buying an SUV and parking it running in the back yard. As an appraiser, I would value our pool at half of cost. Above ground pools are not given any value by the VA. A pool may be worth zero to a person over 65.

Choosing a Realtor

If you are going to try to sell a property yourself for a few weeks and then list it, it is probably better to list it right away.

A Realtor is a member of a national organization promoting professionalism and efficiency. All members must be registered real estate brokers or salesmen.

Don't call your brother-in-law or friend. Realtors are everywhere, but you want one experienced in your neighborhood. Talk to your neighbors, ride the area looking for signs and read the ads looking for listings near yours.

Clean your place up before the Realtor arrives. Turn on all lights and unlock all doors. Secure pets and instruct your agent on how to deal with them after he lists your house.

Invite several agents, but not at the same time. They will give you a free market analysis indicating what your home might be worth.

Once you have listed, help the agent all you can. Refer prospects to him or her. Leave when she is showing your home.

I was showing a small house and the sellers followed us around. There were three people talking to the poor buyer and we bunched in the hall and no one could move.

Measure your own house or have an appraiser do it. Realtors usually take the sq. ft. off the tax card or survey. Recently I appraised a house that sold based on a 100 sq. ft. shortage, costing the seller $2,000.

Be careful about allowing a lock box if you still live there. A lock box holds the key to your house and all Realtors have access. They are great if the house is vacant. Leave the power and water on. Check your vacant house often for open doors or water left running.

Be helpful and encourage caravans and open houses. A caravan is when many Realtors look at your home. Leave during both of these events. Make sure your house goes in multiple listing. This gives hundreds of member agents access to your listing. Most listing contracts are for 90 days or more. Some Realtors will start in right away hammering your price down. You should have a realistic price on it from the beginning and stay with it. A weak seller may get hammered when the Realtor should be hammering the buyer to come up!

Realtors shine in those special situations where the market needs a lubricant. Realtors represent rich buyers keeping their identity secret. I sold a gas station to a neighboring bank who never knew the owner just had a coronary.

Laws are always changing and selling real estate can involve you in a complicated morass. The Realtor usually earns his commission in the same way a truck driver adds value by bringing produce to your table.

Next to a call from your doctor, saying you're pregnant, the most important call is from your Realtor, saying, "You've got the house."

Cut-Rate Brokers

Cut-rate brokers and buy-owner services have proliferated. The mortgage industry is helping the Buy Owner people organize and present their home. It makes a good partnership.

Assist2Sell sells your house for $2,995. They have the ad, "Friends don't let friends pay 6%." A franchise cost $14,000 in 2003 and $19,000 in 2004. Assist2Sell overcomes the lower commission by volume and group advertising.

Assist2Sell gives information on other listings on the back of the data sheet. This "double marketing" is great. The data sheet on the home is placed in plastic tubes/boxes by the sign or inside the home.

A selling broker was refused their normal three percent by an Assist2Sell client. This spreads confusion and bad will.

The recently passed "do not call" law puts limits on Realtors calling FSBOs (for sale by owners). FSBOs have their own TV show like the Realtors, but the Realtors have an entire channel. The real estate channel closed in Jacksonville in 2011.

Realtors puff values up, hoping to get the listing and cover the commission. Cut-rate brokers don't have this incentive as they are mainly order takers.

The cut-rate brokers have failed before, but now not. The difference is the internet and technology.

Buy Owner has TV ads showing a pleased seller who just saved $12,000 in commissions saying, "Thanks, Buy Owner."

The by-owner may have a Realtor drop in or call from the car, wanting to show the home. I recommend the seller cooperate and offer 2 or 3% if a sale results.

Ads

The ad said "Call after 6 PM", those people need a Realtor. Another said: New, never lived in. Another: Townhouse -flat. My favorite is: Appraised $2.95 million, sacrifice for $1.95 million. There's: Upgraded with contemporary styling. (Hard to do) Have someone else read your ad before placing it.

Realtors are allowed to "Puff the goods." What is beautiful is subjective. Neighborhood stretch tries to extend high values into so-so areas. Address inflation happens when they advertise a modest house as being in an expensive area or sometimes give an area both names.

Digital photography and programs like Photoshop allow one to "take out" offensive power lines or even sewer treatment plants. This could be fraud.

A brochure gave a house a concrete porch, which was just a patio. It exclaimed Dining room/Den! Like that was a good thing. Either you don't have a den or don't have a dining room. The ad lauded: Home office or leisure room! (Bedroom without a closet).

The ad said: Serious inquiries only. Another mistake is: Firm. These phrases denote an unfriendly seller or even a hostile one. Put your first and last name in the ad. Ads that say "Call Joe" sound crude or illicit.

Classified ads quicken the pulse. Anytime the entrepreneur doesn't have enough to do, ads bring new prospects to light, and you might turn a profitable deal.

The price was $109,734. This person is probably a "technical" and won't negotiate. Calling this person is apt to be disappointing.

Favorite real estate words are: Nestled, redecorated, spacious, attractive, desirable, modern, new, sparkling, lovely, sunny, beautiful view, luxurious, charmer, sizzling, carriage house, newer, all the bells and whistles, neutral colors and the good earth. Better than new can be true as there are now blinds, fans, etc. Cozy means small and Cottage means real small.

A condominium brochure stated during the slowdown of 2007, "Moving at a slower pace on purpose."

Facebook users are doing their own ads with video of the entire house. The internet offers ad bonanzas, but they have to be constantly maintained.

The ad lauded tile floors as being allergy fighting. They also echo and break dropped glasses.

Signs

As a kid, I loved the Burma Shave signs. Spaced out over about a mile, they really cut boredom on a long trip. They contained a poem ending with "Burma Shave." Also good was "See Rock City" painted on top of a barn by Clark Byers.

Doc. Thornton was an old-fashioned dentist with an office in his home. He worked on blacks and poor people, using a foot pedal drill. I painted a sign for his entrance and was paid $5. It hung there for the next 20 years until he retired.

The most successful sign is the Golden Arches. They started out as part of the McDonald's building and evolved into signs with two golden arches along with the number of burgers sold. They were a result of the McDonald brothers wanting an "M" for each of them at the building ends.

Billboards were on four or five telephone poles, but now are on huge steel tubing, which can withstand everything but a direct hit by a tornado.

As a landowner, they pay you a nice rent, and you don't have to do a thing. Some surplus parcels and remainders from partial takings are only good for billboards.

Signs inform, educate, and amuse. Tom Trout, a local contractor, has inspirational messages on his sign next to 1-95. He changes the message periodically.

Portable yellow flashing signs were rolled out in front of businesses. These usually had yellow bulbs around the edge and were outlawed in Jacksonville in 1992, but LCD screens are now being litigated.

The sign is a great tool for selling real estate. Once in place, it costs nothing, and every sign call has seen the property, so they are pre-qualified.

Bill Watson has had the same sign since he opened in 1960. A blue "Watson" covers a red United States on a white background. Red, white and blue. It has worked, for this sales leader.

Maronda Builders had a billboard indicating their block homes can't have termites. This is a lie, as block homes have much wood framing.

A great idea was the hanging Century 21 yellow and gold sign. These huge signs needed a truck crew for installation, but had a high recognition factor and bonded together all the broker members.

Signage should be simple and easy to read. Avoid purple script on black, or pink roman on white signs that are totally illegible from a moving car.

Which property is the sign on? Often it is placed near the line and you're not sure what is for sale.

Fast sign shops now offer great signs, a big improvement over the old days. Skip the 50-cent tin sign and go with large custom lettering and big phone numbers.

The stronger the seller's market is, the smaller your sign can be.

Illegal, cheap signs are placed in street right-of-ways and corners pointing toward the house for sale.

Information tubes near the For Sale signs aid in selling, and cut down on unqualified calls. Put the info tube close to the street or they will drive in your yard to get the info sheet.

Some Realtors put magnetic signs on their cars, but if you are prone to yell and shake your fist at other drivers, rethink the sign on the car.

One Times Square is where they drop the ball on New Year's Eve. Billboards bring in more rent than the offices inside. (*One Thousand New York Buildings* by Bill Harris)

Signs are expensive and pay taxes to local governments, as well as federal tax on the income they generate. Most require a building permit.

Commercial or business signs blown down in storms can stay that way for months. They are vulnerable, expensive, and hard to fix. Some businesses never fix them.

Murals on buildings are popular and may disguise vacancy. These arty endeavors depict the area's history or attributes, like Jaguars by Jim Draper or Terry Smith's work in Palatka.

Signs are instruments of privacy and safety. Builders use them to keep thieves off site. Owners use them to discourage unwanted visitors. Signs proclaim security systems, whether they exist or not.

In 1973, Bud the sign man had one paint brush and a squalid shop in a poor neighborhood. In 1975 he had an idea: make United States flags for the 1976 Bicentennial. There was a huge run on flags and he was one of a few suppliers and became a rich man.

House Hazards

A huge house existed in my subdivision. It started out as an ordinary house but was added to over the years to reach almost 4,000 sq. ft.

Its value never rose as the maintenance was so high. The last owners had seven children, one of whom left a candle burning at night. The home burned and stood for years a blackened hulk. Pity the neighbors.

Joe built a house in Mandarin. The Interstate 295 and Buckman Bridge was then built, changing the drainage of the area. Joe sold to Earl. Earl found his den flooded every time it rained. Earl, being industrious, built a cow catcher screen porch adjacent to the den, keeping water out.

Houses at risk include those next to curves and at the top of "T" intersections. One house on a four-lane curved road repeatedly got hit by speeding cars so the city erected a barrier and blinker light.

Two different "T" intersections have homes hit by cars. In both cases the straight road is over a mile long and stops just short of the victim house. Amtrak leveled two houses in Palatka. The speeding train left the tracks at 71 MPH in a 35 MPH rated area.

Homes at the bottom of hills can flood during heavy rains. Homes can flood from stopped up storm drains. Grass grows in the ditch and heavy rains bring water into homes which may or may not have flood insurance.

Jacksonville has many military air flights and bases. Some homes are in runway zones and carry higher risk from crashes and others require extra insulation because of noise.

Girvin Road landfill in Jacksonville opened in 1974. This 150-acre site was well located in an area popular with developers.

A developer started a subdivision across the street. Values were discounted because there was a garbage dump nearby. Many people bought, knowing the dump would fill up and close.

The dump didn't close. It grew from 40' to 50' high. Sales slowed to a trickle. The odor was terrible. Thousands of birds swarmed around looking for edibles. They crapped on the homes and dropped garbage on them.

Hundreds of garbage trucks used Girvin Rd. dropping debris, some of which flattened tires of passenger cars.

Today the landfill is closed and topped off with grass. Values are normal, but I wonder about seepage and poisons.

Watch Your Builder

Most builders are good, but construction is complicated and you should watch them as much as possible.

Don't buy off plans without seeing a built version. You can't tell everything from a plan.

Ask for a pre-construction discount. Ask for the broker's discount, about 3%. Buy the model home. You will have to wait for access, but should get all the extras for free.

Plans can be flipped and doors and windows put in upside down. Trusses (roof supports) are leaned against a tree, warping them. Your nails will pop out and there will be leaks.

Kitchen cabinets were leaned against the garage wall and were installed warped. The buyer had to threaten suit to get them replaced.

Be careful buying a plan like the model. Builders take off doors and install mirrors to make the place look bigger.

Avoid the high vaulted ceiling. They are poorly insulated, hard to clean and hot.

The hall is gone. Master bedrooms now open directly onto living space. You have to make the bed before opening the door. Not all plans have it this way.

Buy the largest house you can afford and determine if it is expandable. Can you add on easily?

Buy the last house in the subdivision. The builder may deep discount to get out of there. Ask the builder to hold a fast payout note himself or take something in trade.

Get a two-color fiberglass roof and plant trees right away. Don't change your mind during construction unless you are prepared to pay plenty extra. The architectural shake roof is now popular.

Make friends with the salesman. They often have no builder loyalty and will level with you about problems. Don't buy that one for example, it rained on it during construction for a month.

The garage should be 20' x 20' or larger. Less than that and you have a one car garage: especially with the sport utility vehicles popular today. Kelli's conversion van was too tall to fit in their garage.

If the commode is in its own room, be sure it has a window. A vent fan is not enough. Be sure the shower is large enough. Some are suitable only for a child.

The kitchen is now open to the rest of the house. This requires you to be neat and suffer with noise from dishwashers.

Open all the doors. Sometimes they hit or restrict movement. Some doors are only two feet wide and some people are bigger than that.

A large walk-in closet should have its own air duct and should be distant from the shower to avoid humidity and moisture.

The laundry room should be well drained. A lower floor level with center drain will limit flooding. The water heater should also be in a drained area.

Some builders skip the ceiling light and front porch. You may not notice these right away. The stoop has given way to the diverter, a strip of metal on the eave above the door.

Bad builders hate appraisers. I caught one builder shorting the plan by two feet.

The volume builder may pinch down on his subcontractors so badly that quality suffers. One builder's homes need paint from the very beginning. The painting sub was forced to water down the paint. If a disreputable builder fails to pay his subs, you may have to. Check on your builder's reputation and don't pay him in advance.

Drinking can be a problem. Look over your site for miniatures or beer cans. Be careful not to step on a roofing nail. They have one inch square heads and can stand straight up.

Ask if trusses can be selected to give you a real stand up attic. Off grade homes are a thing of the past but they sure make it easier to work on plumbing, electric and so on. Be careful about a jet tub upstairs. Vibrations can loosen the ceiling of the room below or allow leaking.

If you see something that bothers you during construction, speak up. It's much easier to fix sooner rather than later. Construction of a house is like the birth of a baby. You should be there all the time.

PUDs

PUDS are planned unit developments. This was a zoning concept that preplanned all aspects of the project. Sometimes they were mixed use, combining offices with residences and stores.

Today, they mean a subdivision with a mandatory owner's fee. A neighborhood association is made up of people from the development company and later is turned over to the residents. The association enforces the deed restrictions.

The PUD usually has a perimeter fence and magnificent entrance. Some have divided entry roads with one lane per direction. This is dangerous if a car breaks down and blocks traffic.

There are common grounds, landscaping, woods set aside and parks. There might be trails, playgrounds, and, in some cases, shopping areas in the middle of a large PUD. Amenities include lakes, ponds, pools, tennis courts, clubhouse, and entry guard.

The guard can be a person or an automated electric gate Punch in the code and the gate opens. The gates are frustrating when people forget the code and keep punching until something happens. Their car can run out of gas, or break down, and access to an entire project is thwarted. To breach the security gate, wait for a car to arrive and follow it inside.

PUDs are safe and have been a good investment. However, if dominated by one or a few builders, they can be monotonous. Narrow lots create a one house look and if they have mailboxes it can look like a fence.

All gated communities are PUDs (or condos), but not all PUDs have gates. Electric gates have taken on a negative image as some crime ridden apartments now have them.

PUD fees are usually paid quarterly or annually. They run with the land and are applicable to vacant lots. Tim once took a PUD lot in trade for a debt and was angered to learn of accumulated fees of $3,000. (Late fees may compound and become confiscatory.)

The home can be taken, as in foreclosure, for non-payment of these fees. Late charges and attorney's fees escalate the debt. One association manager absconded with the cash, throwing the PUD into chaos.

Transition from developer to owner management may be troublesome. Men with no business experience manage a 400 home community. Often, there isn't a quorum (minimum needed to make a decision).

An energetically managed PUD tries to kill the slob in all of us. Tires: $ fine, bad paint: $ fine, window air conditioner: $ fine. Understandably, wars result; Tom painted his house pink, and Bill filled his yard with rocks.

A PUD from hell went too far when they prohibited the flying of the American flag. The court ruled in favor of the homeowner.

Garry Trudeau's Doonesbury ran a strip about homeowner's associations arresting people who hung their wash out to dry. (My parents never owned a washer or dryer.)

Some homes are abandoned. The grass grows and pieces rot and fall off. The homeowner's association has limits.

PUD restrictions include: Don't leave your garage door open and you can't have trucks or vehicles with writing on them.

The most universal trait of PUDs is fee creeping. If the fee is $100/year, next year it will be $110, the year after it will be $120, and so on.

Builders are shrinking lot sizes. They point to the amenities, common greenery and wooded parks, and say you don't need a big lot. A 3,000 sq. ft. home sits on a 60-foot lot.

The house above, if one-story, would have a 3,000 sq. ft. foot print. Small lots pressure homes to go upward. A two-story house of 3,000 sq. ft. would probably have a 1,500 sq. ft. footprint, increasing yard space.

The small lots require "clear-cutting," or stripping the land of all trees. You get an impression of trees, however, from the set-aside green areas. Commonly owned trees are better than nothing.

Mail delivery should be at your door. The cluster boxes look cheap and cause traffic snarls. One project had brick mail boxes every 60 feet (small lots) and a narrow street. It looked like hundreds of soldiers lined up for roll call. Nothing trashes an otherwise nice neighborhood like a bunch of cheap leaning mailboxes.

Mail delivery can be changed from the door to a box. The post office has retrofitted some areas to save on costs or speed delivery.

PUD values may be slow to rise. As the builder is in competition with you for many years, you may not be able to sell your house. A downturn means the builder cuts prices below what you paid. The builder has sales staff and mortgage personnel on site. You will have to give away your drapes, fans and wallpaper to compete.

You paid $200,000 for a 2,500 sq. ft. home, only to find new 1,800 sq. ft. homes are selling for $150,000.

Once the builder sells out, values can spurt up. Re-sales may reflect owner improvements or the lack of competing projects nearby.

Be careful about buying next to the perimeter. PUD developers have no control over what happens outside, and you may someday be looking at the back of a store, apartment complex, or church with spotlight.

Sometimes PUDs dissolve. In middle class subdivisions so many residents may not pay that it tips toward undoing. A project should have over 100 lots to spread the cost.

PUDs have done better retaining value with the 2011 recession than non PUDs, as a general rule.

Gates Keep Value in and Slobs Out

Gated communities have prestige and offer a controlled environment. They should reduce stress and increase order in an executive's frantic life.

Prestige makes people move into large homes they can't afford. Soon they are anxious to sell and other buyers wanting prestige buy them. Some luxury markets are very active, which in a way lowers prestige.

Deerwood was developed by the Skinner family in the '60's. They never intended it to be expensive, but during the development stage muck was found, so the price went up to cover removal costs.

Bill Sutton of Safe Touch Security says a gated community was victimized by the minimum wage guards, who had radios and knew who was coming and going, in or out. Guards give a false sense of security, and cause people to leave doors unlocked----- very unwise.

Motorcycles became more respectable, so the rules were softened in The Woods. A woman got in trouble over having 9 cats in Jacksonville Golf and Country Club. An old widow was evicted when she failed to pay PUD fees and the association foreclosed. A lawsuit was filed over uncut grass in Chimney Lakes.

Fences and gates can only do so much. True, they keep value in, but if you can buy a comparable property for half the price outside of the project, it might be time to rethink the PUD's significance.

Queen's Harbor allowed an estate sale. Estelle Medlock talked to the PUD manager, who did a straw poll, called a few people and no one objected. During the sale, some residents did object, but it was too late. Now such sales are held by appointment.

PUDs micro-manage our behavior and boost prestige. A South Florida PUD tried to keep out O.J. Simpson. Homeowners' associations must be listed with the State of Florida, Division of Corporations.

There are no slums on golf courses. Many PUDs have golf courses. Jacksonville scored a coup when World Golf Village located here in 1997. Courses sometimes convert to subdivisions, as in St. Augustine. It takes a huge amount of water to keep them green. Some neighbors get hit by golf balls if their house is unfortunately located.

Save Energy- Go Green

Mrs. Jean owned a cottage behind her house. She cut a wire into the line before it reached the meter and received free electricity for the cottage for years. Theft of electricity is quite common.

Al Gore, energy guru, owns a 20-room house with 8 bathrooms which consumes 20 times the national average of energy for American homes. It is near Nashville, Tennessee.

Ask the builder about their insulation standards. R-11 in the walls and R-19 in the ceiling is a minimum. Ask about the air condenser. Most builders give you a 10-seer unit when you should have a 12-seer unit. Get double pane windows. Minimum electric service is 150 amps. Two hundred amps costs a little more and is better.

A solar hot water heater costing $3,300 saves a family of five about $40/month on their electric bill. This is a return of 14.5% per year:

$40 x 12 mos. = $480/yr., divided by $3,300 = 14.5%

Tank-less hot water heaters have advantages that save energy. They cost more than regular heaters, but last longer. Water is heated only when needed. James Dulley is the expert: www.Dulley.com.

Ceramic insulating paint will reflect significant heat from the house's exterior.

Stress skin panel homes have R factors as high as 50. They are load bearing and recommended by James Dulley.

Why do we set the thermostat on 70 in the summer and 80 in the winter? Maybe it's fear of heat or cold.

The attic should be insulated and vented. Light-colored shingles reflect more sunlight, saving energy. Use window awnings to cut sun and add accent.

Weather-strip doors and windows. Use ceiling fans in lieu of air conditioning. The attic fan or whole house fan is an overlooked asset. Energy doors are insulated, steel skinned. Ridge vents let the attic breathe and reduce hot air and moisture.

A stylish ridge vent is the cupola, with vents, and weather vane. They're cute, but vulnerable during high winds.

Shade the air compressor from direct sun. Install a pet door instead of waiting for a cat to saunter in with door open.

Stylish high ceilings cost more to build, heat and cool. Fluorescent bulbs save over incandescent ones.

With imported oil being a political and military flashpoint, individual savings of energy is important. We should put little windmills on our houses to generate power. All of us should peddle on electric generating bikes.

During the energy crunch of '81, ceiling fans boomed. Retrofitted fans wobble, but endure. A $29 fan looks awful. Small bedrooms might benefit from fans with clear blades.

A surprising number of people live "off grid" or with no electric service. They thrive with propane, batteries, generators, solar, insulation, and ingenuity. Remote acreage can support dozens of homes sharing some facilities.

Insulate the garage door. Proper sealing can also keep out rain and water. Insulate the entire garage, especially if it used to be a carport and you have access to the walls during construction.

Many PUD association managers prohibit solar panels due to appearance. States are passing laws to overturn this anomaly. Even city planning departments have prohibited them.

Additions

Adding on to the house must be popular, so many people do it. We would not have bought our home on Acapulco Rd. without the addition. Our addition is indistinguishable from the original construction. The materials and style are the same. The only clue is the thick wall where the door is. This used to be an outside wall. The roof leaked where our addition joins the house. The added den has custom built-in bookcases. A properly done addition is a thing of beauty and makes the house unique.

Hire an architect. Buy a computer program to help in design. If you can't match materials and design, consider a completely different addition concept from the original.

Give written specifications to the contractor. They don't like to write things down and some can't write. It will also help with competitive bidding, since each builder will bid the same work. Additions often don't add their full cost to value.

Beware the glass sun room. They look good in magazines but in Florida can turn into humid ovens. They leak and turn brown.

Add in! Improve the space you've already got.

Fill in porches. Altama Rd. had a roof over a walkway surrounded by sand. For $100 we got concrete poured, which tripled value over cost in 1969.

Acapulco Rd. had a screen porch. Kim's Afghan hound jumped through the screen and got run over. We glassed in this porch and ducted it, costing $3,500 or $25 a sq. ft., but value went up to $50 a sq. ft.

An atrium is a "hole in the house." It is a "skylight" surrounded by walls and glass. Sliding glass doors open so you can water plants. One guy roofed his atrium and poured a floor, picking up 100 sq. ft. and making a dining area.

Sapelo Rd. had a double carport added in front of the original single garage. This is an ideal situation to make the garage into living area, as no value is lost due to lost car covering.

Bob's garage got crushed by snow. The one story garage joined the two story house. Insurance money rebuilt the garage and he boosted height and cut a door off his master bedroom and made a room above the garage. The out of pocket cost was $25 a sq. ft. but value added was $50 a sq. ft.

Adding up is possible, but tricky and expensive. The big lot is great for detached buildings and mother-in-law apartments. A business bought the house next door and joined it into the first house in commercial zoning.

Adding is risky and can crack existing walls or slabs. Some contractors specialize in adding on. The tax assessor gets copies of the permit so they don't miss your improvement.

Conversion and Value Loss

Conversion is a change in use; say from a house to an office. This often requires little alteration to the building.

Many old fashioned gas stations have been converted, but those pump islands or the raised concrete platforms remain. The oil company should remove the gasoline tanks after closing one of their stations.

Convenience stores convert well because they are just a box. One became a church. Train stations become convention centers and the train can be a hotel. A wonderful church in

Charleston, South Carolina, was changed into a restaurant. A wooden factory became shrimp boats.

A 12-sided concrete gas tank in Palatka was converted into nice office space. Many vacant stores now become antique consignment malls. A mini-warehouse bay became a residence; of course, that was illegal.

Conversion saves historic architecture. This is also restoration. The Eros Theater of Love became first class office space. An old hotel with turret was a brothel, then a residence and now an attorney's office.

Land use converts, too. Often the appraiser's dilemma is estimating the highest and best use. A trailer park is changed into a shopping center site. The residents are displaced, but land value is validated. The mini-warehouse banks some land until it is ready for better. Rural land changing into anything alarms many environmentalists.

Some things can't be converted, like a waterslide. For these, demolition is the way. All properties can be changed into parking lots. Value slips away over time and demolition admits the value is zero. If you tear down a building, tell the tax assessor so he can take it off your bill.

The fish camp had an unfinished block structure which I helped demolish. I was amazed at how easily the block pulverized with a hammer and how hard it was to clean up afterward.

When I was six there was a factory behind our house in Ohio. It belched black smoke and filled the sky. It scared me so I went inside, pulled all the blinds and pretended it was night.

This is economic depreciation: a loss in value occurring from an outside cause. Wars and political strife cause economic depression. The Gulf War emptied many Jacksonville houses, stopped the market and lowered values. We are a Navy town.

In 1984 a fired security guard walked into a McDonalds and shot and killed 21 customers. McDonalds tore the building down in an effort to remove all traces of extreme negativity.

Putnam County ruined land values when they passed an impact fee of about $1,000. This is a onetime charge when you built a home or set up a trailer. The market for cheap lots went to zero and owners stopped paying taxes. The county then owned thousands of tax deeds.

The most common form of economic depreciation probably comes from neighbors. Barking dogs, pink fences, Hell's Angels, un-cut grass, rodents, radios; the list is endless.

Functional or design obsolescence results when a feature is ill conceived or outdated. Included here are small closets, small kitchens, out-of-date heat or wiring and the big daddy of them all, the bad addition.

The bad addition can cause a value loss. Dens added onto dens, poorly built or filled in rooms can look like a LSD trip. Home Depot and others have made handymen out of weekend beer drinkers.

Most property just runs down or wears out. This is physical deterioration. Left un-repaired, damage can escalate rapidly. A roof leaks and at first there is just a spot on the ceiling; then all of a sudden the whole ceiling falls in. Wiring looks bad, but value loss is low until the fire happens.

Failure to paint the exterior is a common cause of sheet rot. Leaking plumbing can rot an entire foundation. The tip of the iceberg principle applies.

Malls, Stores and Shopping Centers

There were no malls when I was a boy. Only the multistory department store downtown. After World War II, cars increased and shopping centers stole downtown's thunder. Stores followed the homes.

Before malls there was the strip center. The first strip center was a Seven-11 with added stores.

I moved to Jacksonville, Florida in 1967. My boss, Earl, showed me around and we had lunch at Regency Square Mall, the first enclosed shopping mall I had ever seen. I wasn't in Palatka anymore!

Back then, it was 60 stores, .and has now grown to 1.4 million sq. ft. with 130 stores. It is almost a mile long.

Martin Stein and Alexander Brest had vision and daring. They developed the mall on mined sand dunes. Not only was the location in "the middle of nowhere," but the sand was like the Sahara Desert. Charlie Basset, a surveyor, showed them how to build on the land.

Regency Square was Jacksonville's first regional mall. A regional mall is the largest and draws customers from a 100-mile wide radius. It pulled many other stores and businesses with it. Regency had a few nice restaurants, but none have lasted. Theme restaurants surround the mall property.

In 1981 Regency was enlarged. The architecture blended well, but required a lowered ceiling in the old part. Most storefronts in the old part were extended forward about six feet to use up part of the too-wide walkway. Skylights were built or retrofitted, as styling accent and protection against daytime blackout, although this increased air conditioning bills.

The mall is a major achievement, enclosing and covering shopping, with adjacent parking. No wonder downtown lost out.

Kiosks are mobile booths placed in malls, which allow small businessmen to sell jewelry, cigars, etc. Unmanned kiosks are similar to billboards. They pay rent of $1,000 per month or more.

Malls have shows to attract customers: cars, art, antiques, models, toys, etc. Some have performers and health check-ups. I took Dad to the Palatka Mall for a free screening. Malls may also offer motor home and camping hookups.

Some malls have kiddie centers: supervised play areas where you can drop the kids, paying an hourly rate.

The busiest part of a mall is often the food court.

New malls have an advantage. Shoppers will pass by an older mall to get to a new one where it is perceived the stores are better and more "chic".

Mini-malls at airports are doing well. Increased time to get cleared for security has given mall tenants more time to make sales. Malls are for the young. Teens are dropped off and "date" at malls. Hundreds of no-money teens roam mall corridors looking at their peers.

Is the mall out of date? Developers think it's cheaper to cluster buildings together with fancy fronts. The fronts can be offset giving the impression of separate buildings. Parking can be closer to one's destination.

Power centers are large shopping centers with one or more national tenants. Whether it's called a town center, lifestyle center or Main Street village, the trend is to take the top off.

St. Johns Town Center in Jacksonville looks like an old-fashioned downtown or Disneyland and is the "hot" center.

Shopping center developers are getting better at leaving trees in the parking lots. This really helps the view.

Wal-Mart, the big store or big box, can build a 5-acre store for $30 per sq. ft. Many chain stores "adopt" a contractor and get deep discounts for the volume business.

Wal-Mart has modified some store designs to better fit in to certain communities. Critics say, "It's like putting a tuxedo on Frankenstein."

Five and dime stores have been replaced by dollar stores. These and drive-through pharmacies are all the rage in 2011.

The worst traffic is often near the mall. Excess traffic can strangle and cut off access to your business. Bypasses, flyovers, overpasses and road widening are all likely to be built.

Gas Pains

Remember when they came out to your car and you said "Fill'er up". In 1973 the oil sheiks got together and embargoed the sale of cheap gas. Gas lines formed and irate customers fumed. It is better to have expensive gas than no gas at all.

The old fashioned traditional station was doomed. Retailers dumped them by the thousands. I appraised many of them for Standard Oil, Gulf and Phillips 66.

Seven-11 kicked off the convenience store craze. Pay more, but get quick shopping. The average store was 2,500 sq. ft. During the steep recession of 1981, government bonds allowed 100% financing for new stores and I appraised hundreds of them for many c-store owners.

Gas made them more valuable. Today the old fashioned station and c-store have merged and you can even get fried chicken, tacos or donuts (no wonder we are fat). Today's store is 5,000 sq. ft, and needs a half acre or more. Boldly lit, they are downtown to many small towns.

Buy next to one of these stores. Most do well and will want to expand adding a barber shop or boutique of some kind.

Some of the best bargains in this book were sold by gas retailers after 1973. The St. Augustine exit off 1-95 is a prime location. The oil company sold an acre site in 1975 for $35,000 and it was bought by McDonald's in 1982 for $350,000 a return of 33% per annum.

Buy at major interstate interchanges.

In 1974 pump your own gas began. I was shocked at the degree of trust this implied, but it has stayed with us by paying in advance.

Lodging

We packed the 1948 Olds 88 with everything we owned. It was black, four-door with red interior and automatic select radio. I stood up on the front floor and my head cleared the roof. I lay down on the parcel shelf behind the back seat during long trips.

After dark we stopped and inspected the motel room. Mother found a roach so we kept going. There were no more rooms until we found a truck stop and stayed above a restaurant.

Holiday Inn introduced the room you could trust to be nice and clean.

In high school I stayed at the New York Plaza. I was on a school trip staying at the New Yorker when Conrad called. He was in the middle of steel negotiations, but I saw him one night.

I put on my only suit, a brown metallic. I showed up at the Plaza and Conrad congratulated me on my suit and showed me up to his room. I hardly saw him anymore, but ordered room service and spread my postcards out on the bed. I opened the window overlooking Central Park and listened to thousands of horns and sirens.

The suit was exactly like one I had seen Little Richard wear, but by 11th grade I had acquired a normal dark one.

In 1993 we went to St. Louis to see the arch and stayed at the old train station hotel next to a shopping mall. My first experience with a jet tub was in a hotel in St. Petersburg, Florida. The Peachtree in Atlanta has an exterior glass elevator which rides up 70 floors.

The Suites Hotel has room for children in the living room while adults have privacy in the bedroom. We stayed at the Sands in Las Vegas, but not in the tower. There was a regular motel attached to the tower.

Almost all motel rates are negotiable. Tell them you are on business or part of a group. Disney World area hotels in Orlando are very competitive, but they rip you on little things like charging for ice. On the grounds, Disney hotels are so expensive they don't have to do that.

The extended stay hotel is a new idea and many units now offer kitchenettes. The lines between hotels and apartments are blurred. Free breakfast, internet connection and exercise room are standard.

Timeshares have value in places like Disney or Key West, which are truly unique and always stay rented. Most time shares are not worth their price.

Duval Appraising

Jacksonville occupies most of Duval County thanks to consolidation of county and city governments in 1967. The city is over 800 sq. miles. This huge tax base keeps taxes low.

Open all mail. In 1975 the VA (Veterans Administration) sent out a broker mass mail. "Sorry we are slow with appraisals, we are behind due to unprecedented work load." Rocket scientist that I am, I applied to be a VA appraiser and was accepted.

A worn house sells at a discount. Makes sense until they find out the VA appraisal is as repaired. VA does not require cosmetic repairs; only those necessary to make the house safe, sound and sanitary, but still the seller gets low-balled due to condition and then has to fix the place up to comply with VA.

Duval can't compare to Putnam County for colorful appraisals, but I did do a topless bar. I also found a body behind a convenience store. It turned out to a passed out drunk.

One of my subjects got in the newspaper. A funeral home was assigned to me as an SBA (Small Business Administration) repossession. It was dark and I saw broken windows and flies. I did not know there were bodies stuffed everywhere. The owner was arrested for violation of health and burial laws.

I pulled up for the inspection. A kid was holding a large snarling dog at the end of a rope. The kid was losing ground and might let go of the rope at any moment, so I left and went back later.

An owner came home and I had left the door open from the house to the garage. He got right in my face and screamed about his air conditioning bill. Coincidentally, the comparable sales did not justify his sale price.

I opened the bedroom door. The repossession appraisal was of a vacant house. A cat had been closed up, screamed and flew past my head. My heart was thumping.

Another repo had teen boys getting high and another had drunks passed out on the floor. Some repos have so much stuff left behind you can't see the floor.

Al Kafer was my insurance agent. He retired and I appraised his home. He was personable and home all the time, so he was available to show the place. He received full price and in cash. He paid no broker and no loan fees. Almost no by-owners have an appraisal to guide the buyer.

Roland Richardson was a good repeat client. He owned the Biskits chain for a while. He bought closed restaurants, fixed them up, resold them or opened them for business. You won't be hungry if you look in the kitchen.

One day we met in his attorney's office to start a job. He hadn't seen me in a while and boomed "You've got jowls." I wasn't sure what he meant and later disagreed. Lunch was brought in. Not used to wearing a tie, it went in the soup.

Palatka Past and Gone

While I was at the University of Florida, Dad got me a VW bug for my 21st birthday. I had an Impala convertible picked out, but he was all for saving on gas. It was a 1963 brand new model with everything except a sunroof. I stopped short of ordering that, but even so the price was a walloping $1,800. VW did not negotiate their prices and I was lucky to get them to pay attention to me at all since at age 21, I looked about 14. It even had seat belts which gathered dust.

One night coming back from Orlando, I neared the St. Johns River and Palatka. I had been down there taking my real estate test for the Florida salesman exam. I flunked it the first time. Since I had been to 2 classes on real estate at the University of

Florida, I saw no need to study the handbook. The second time I had the law memorized and passed it easily.

An orange glow could be seen and when I got on the bridge I could see the wall of flame engulfing the old Security Feed and Seed place on the river by the bridge. The powdery feed blew up several times. Years later a Holiday Inn was built on this site.

On the other side of the bridge in 1969, an entire block of old buildings was removed to make way for a HUD 7-story apartment. Dad and I appraised this block, which included the Palatka Daily News and Howell Theater. I delivered papers as a boy and never knew the theater was integrated. Blacks went up to the balcony to watch movies. They had their own concession stand and bathrooms. The HUD apartment was torn down in 2009. HUD stands for Housing and Urban Development, an arm of the federal government.

Monty's Restaurant burned as did the New Theater. Neither was rebuilt. The 3-story brick middle school was demolished to make way for local government buildings. Also taken was Baraday's News Stand. This is where I looked at *Sexology* Magazine to learn how reproduction happened. Clark's Hobby

Shop was removed for bank expansion. This is where I bought comic books, models and the 22 rifle used to shoot up the shack. Moore's Drugs came down. This is where my parents and I would meet for coffee.

The ice house and Setzer's Grocery came down. The jail on the river was demolished after much asbestos concern. The James Hotel is still there, but boarded-up. A large office supply store burned. An old river front house was carted off by barge to a new location. Winn Dixie closed, leaving downtown with no grocery store.

George owned many shanties rented to the poor and minorities. When a family would move out, George "sold it to a northern buyer" meaning insurance paid off his fire claim.

The State Road 19 bypass became the new downtown with a Wal-Mart, Chili's and all the new stores and restaurants. Downtown fought back and planted trees, installed benches, brick accent and decorative lighting, but today it is half vacant.

Did Conrad Play God? Yes!

Mother died in 1987 and I cleaned out the house. Dad retired in 1988 and I cleaned out the office. There were thousands of pages of documents, and I learned.

Uncle Conrad was in the 90% income tax bracket in the late '50's and early '60's. Only the top portion of his salary was taxed that high but he lowered his bill by having family businesses.

He'd rather give his money to family than the government.

Dad and Conrad were partners in the fish camp. After that, Dad got a salary of around $500 a month from 1957 to 1967. No wonder Dad did so well in Palatka. I was stunned. Here I'd gone into real estate thinking it was sure fire riches, when all along there had been this subsidy. My parents kept that detail to themselves.

Conrad had a coffee business with my Uncle Gene. Childless, Conrad and Irene raised one of the Gene kids (they had four) from her ninth grade in a Pittsburgh boarding school. I was told that they wanted me, but my parents would not turn loose of their only child.

Conrad had a cattle and land business with my Uncle Kenneth. This made money due to land appreciation. Kenneth was brilliant, but argumentative and no business man.

The IRS was all over Conrad who was audited frequently. He supported Irene's two old unmarried sisters, one with a book store business, apartment above and the other finally moved in with Conrad and Irene.

Dad was as generous with me as Conrad had been with him. In 1987 he gave me $10,000 from a maturing certificate of deposit. The Palatka bank clerk's jaw dropped. "You're just going to give him all that?" Small town banks were anything but impersonal. After giving me the money, Dad told me what to do with it for months.

As Mother aged and got feisty, she hated Conrad and claimed he played God. Conrad gave me $100 for every "A" I got during my last two years in high school. It took him months to pay the $700.

I told my chums stories about flying around in his company plane. He permeated our lives and influenced where we lived and thus who I married. To Dad and me he was a god.

Dad the Broker

Dad liked people and was good talker. His realty career started when he was 56. He would attempt a joke, but they often lacked something. He wore white shirt and tie with leaking pens in the pocket. He had disputes, but no enemies. I never saw him in a bad mood and he was always glad to see me.

His best thing was buying a run-down building and fixing it up. There were plenty to pick from in Palatka. He learned about fixing up at the fish camp. He'd shadow repairmen, "helping" them and checking his watch.

He said you never go wrong taking a profit. A few buildings were so bad I talked him out of buying them. Dad was always thinking and he kept me busy thinking about his deals. He never did most of them, so was merely thinking out loud.

He'd say, "Deals are like streetcars, there's always another one coming." I know now Dad was a busyholic. This person has to stay busy and money is secondary.

The pinnacle of Dad's personal selling career came when he sold the judge's house. It was a grand place on the hill, built like a fortress. In 1965 this home sold for an unheard-of price for that time: $50,000. I could scarcely imagine the loftiness of that value. I noticed that this was the only time Dad decided to tithe, as the judge was a church elder.

Dad was judgmental about drinking. He'd tell a drinking client that it was too early for him. He drank when Conrad visited, but only half of one drink. Conrad left dozens of bottles of liquor at our apartment for his next visit. Mother was a teetotaler.

Dad was an aggressive cost cutter and loved low overhead, while I was ambitious. He had a 4-door '61 Pontiac Bonneville. It began to quit running and left him and his customers down a dirt road. The car did it again and again before Dad would pay a mechanic to fix it.

He'd list a furnished house and buy a table for $10. Then pay Prevatt $20 to refinish it. The result was a beautiful table worth $400.

Aldrich worked out of his home or branch office. He was a good producer for 20 years and Dad gave him most of the commission. Mother complained that Dad was too generous.

Long after Aldrich quit, we got sued over a land area discrepancy. This wasn't Aldrich's fault, as Putnam County had some of the worst maps in America back then. Still, it cost $3,500 to settle it. Mother was right after all.

The law says you must keep files 5 years minimum but this case taught me that you'd better keep them forever. Paul and Otha were friendly and productive. Jake was the last associate and he was a high volume producer for us.

Sell It if You Cannot Donate It

Dad survived heart surgery at age 87, but was no longer able to work. Jake was willing to stay on, but I didn't want any more complications than necessary, so I closed our Palatka office. Jake moved in his main client, Huntley Jiffy stores and they became an excellent tenant.

The other side of our office building has been rented to Hutch, a minority grant getter. I cleaned out all of our files in May of 1988.

Dad still liked to go to the office. He'd show me the land corners. He pointed to one corner and said, "Son, buried there is a fuel tank. I sure hope it doesn't cause a problem.

I said, "Don't worry. What problem could it possibly cause?"

Hutch moved in subtenants, but still had trouble paying the rent of $175 month. The building owner beside us put up a sign which said "Parking in Rear". This invited his customers to park on our lot. Some of them left their car running in our driveway while they ran in to buy a hairbrush.

It seems mine wasn't the only buried gas tank in Palatka. Environmental engineers began combing the area and with Hutch's help found my tank. He called me and for the modest sum of $4,700 we could get it removed and clean up any mess. I asked him, "Who gave you the right to trespass?"

Environmental sleuths swarmed over the neighborhood. Some old gas stations had buried tanks in the street. There were so many tanks the street caved in at one point. When I didn't hire the man who found my tank, he reported it to the state.

I had too much to think about with Dad's post operative stress and the 10 properties I now owned, so I thought, "Let's donate the Palatka office." The donation would be worth about $15,000 in saved taxes.

Jake was excited about the donation so we offered it to his church. They were slow to respond and finally said no thanks. Dad was a Methodist, and *they* were slow to respond and finally said no thanks. This was the first time in my career that I saw fear over pollution render a property value zero.

Hutch got later and later with his rent. Finally after four months of arrearage I sued for collection. We had a court date and I got a judgment against him for the back rent and got my space back. I got four bids and the tank was removed for $2,300. There was no pollution to clean up.

Now that there was a vacancy, I received interested calls in the building. Several renters and buyers looked at it. The duplex had been on the market since 1988 for $55,000. It sold for the full price in January 1993, but I had to take the Black Creek lot in trade.

Instead of $15,000 in saved taxes, which would have taken me two years to use up, I now pocketed $35,000 in cash plus the creek lot. It sold in 1997 for $18,000, which paid for Stephanie's wedding.

The timing worked in my favor.   State Road 19 was clobbering downtown and waiting longer to sell this office would have worked against me.

Donate It If You Cannot Sell It

In 1988 I bought a lot behind our Palatka office It was similar to the one I had sold to Coca Cola for $10,000. The price was $3,000. They wanted money for Christmas.

I had control of Dad's money, but since he was never to work again, I was finished, too, but didn't know it in 1988.

Coke left the block in 1990. One of my trees was blown down on top of a neighbor's jeep. People dump garbage on vacant land.

Dad would push his lawn mower down there from Emmett Street, a distance of eight blocks. Sometimes neighbors would help him with a ride.

The office sold in 1993 and this lot was left as a residue. I offered it to the neighbor for $3,000, but no deal. It appraised at $7,500, thanks to the Coke sale and others. I gave it to the nearby Baptist Church and saved $3,000 on my taxes.

The recipient should keep it two years. If it's sold by the recipient during the first two years of their ownership for less than the appraised value, the donor owes taxes on the difference.

This donation flew by the IRS with colors. It was done right and it was a small deal. Donations do invite audits, so have a good accountant.

Be the Banker and Hold the Mortgage

Dad came home from quadruple bypass surgery June 1, 1988. He had survived at age 87 and he lived at 510 Emmett St. for the next six years.

I made the one hour drive from Jacksonville to Palatka once a week during the first year. Round the clock nurses were hired for the first two and a half months.

Neighbors were vital to his well being. Maxine next door and Carol across the street pitched in and helped him wash and cook.

We went to the grocery store and he shined his '77 Olds even though it was rusted through. Mother had died in 1987 and we put plastic flowers on her grave.

My son-in-law used the upstairs toilet and flooded the downstairs. Dad collected dozens of stray cats by feeding them and fleas overran the house. He was convinced water was coming in through a roof vent pipe and hired a neighborhood kid to put a lid on it. The kid climbed out a second floor window and was paid $1.

A woman followed Dad home, pushed him down and took his money. Later, his pistol was stolen and used in a drug deal. He invited wanderers in to eat and they used the phone: long distance.

Dad wanted the roof painted. The steep pitch metal roof was painted with special aluminum paint costing $1,000. I think they started a leak by walking up there. We paid about $500 in plumbing work. I drove to Palatka for most of these events.

Dad began to sell his own house. Deal one materialized and he would be allowed to stay there. We ran credit and crime reports on these people and I signed them up. Then they backed out over a zoning problem.

He sold it again, but this time the buyer's money kept disappearing. By the time a meeting with the attorney happened, his down payment was nonexistent. This guy eventually bought it through the Realtor.

He ordered a termite inspection and said, "We want a real good inspection." The company took that to mean a tent fumigation costing $thousands. It never happened.

Deal three was underway when he fell and had to relocate into a Jacksonville nursing home. In 1994, I listed the house with Ben Bates Realty. They sold it right away for $45,000 and I held the mortgage. I put due on sale in the contract, but that was ignored in the final papers. The home has resold again and again.

I was flooded with offers to buy this mortgage. Every week an out-of-town company wrote or called. The sale went into a national data base. I had no idea buying seller held mortgages was such a big business. They succeed because sellers get tired of being the banker and who could blame them with representation like Bates gave me. Sellers also find many uses for the cash.

The only proof of the mortgage balance with seller-held mortgages is the amortization schedule. This is a computer-generated list of payments broken down as to principal and interest. Each month check off the payment number and put it on your check. Make copies of checks paid and received. Computer programs vary, so be sure the seller and buyer both have the same exact schedule. Over time the interest income can double your sale's price.

Advice and Ideas

If your house doubled in value in four years, you'd think God had chosen you for success. That is what you are doing for the banks when you pay them 18% interest on a credit card. One dollar invested at 18% doubles to $2 in 47 months or 3.9 years.

Save a little money each month. Time is precious and you can't get it back. It and it alone will make you rich because of the magic of compound interest. Live long and prosper!

Dad and Mother saved $10 a week out of his paycheck (Mother never worked after marriage) and by 1950 they had $10,000. During World War II they bought bonds and saved while being patriotic.

Dump the poor investments and get the good ones paid for. It's sad when people keep losing property waiting to be vindicated. If it's losing after five years, chances are it will lose forever.

You own air rights above your land and mineral rights below it. Devices are being built to "look" underground. Buy stock in real estate companies or REIT's (real estate investment trusts).

Buy from divorcing couples, but don't own with an ex-spouse. Be careful about thinking the second deal will work just because the first one did well. The second may bomb. Your spouse is your partner and he or she must support your investment goals.

Keep your purchases affordable. No real estate does well until it is paid off. Listen and learn. Ask questions. Determine seller motivation. Get to know the seller and don't make him mad.

Cater to the dominant spouse when buying. Study the property over time.

Seller responses upon being asked, "Why are you selling?" is amazing. "I'm sick, dying, retired or transferred." There is pollution, noise, crime, family member sick or I just inherited a bundle and could care less about this shack. A motorcycle gang moved in next door or I've lost my job.

Don't sell a location unless you have a much better one to buy. Buy where property is seen on busy streets. Buy on a busy street before the zoning tips toward commercial. Buy near the bypass highway. Buy near a shopping mall.

Get a survey and check the zoning yourself before buying. Be the first one in a small town. Dig a well while it's still legal. Buy unique property. Buy an added-to house and get the extra space for free. Don't pay much for a vacant building.

Donate land if it will help your remaining land. Buy from recipients, as their cost basis is zero. Attend bank sellouts early to get the advertised deal. Ask a real estate salesman what is your best deal. Sell to or buy from your neighbor.

When buying an apartment, confirm the rent with each tenant. Consider your tenant as your partner and take them small gifts at holidays. Ride by your property often.

Ask questions right up to and during closing. One old woman confessed at a closing that river water had once surrounded the house. The buyer took it anyway, a wiser person.

Don't insult the seller's property. This will not drive down the price, but it will make him mad and you will not be able buy from him.

Understand Compound Interest

In 1931, Dad went to a rodeo in the Midwest. He wrestled a bull to the ground and tied him up. For this victory, he was paid $30 in three $10 gold pieces.

He flew in an open bi-plane for $10, bought a pair of beaded Indian moccasins and headdress for $10 and used the rest to get home on.

When I knew him, he was less frivolous with his funds. When I was old enough to understand percentages, he explained compound interest and said if I saved my money, I could earn more money in my sleep.

Put $1,000 in the bank, paying 6% annual interest. At the end of the year you will have $1,060. At the end of the second year, you will have earned 6% on $1,060 and will have $1,124. The interest earned, as long as you don't spend it, looks like this:

End of year one $60.00

End of year two $63.60

End of year three $67.42

Notice the increase gets bigger. That is because you are getting paid interest on the previous year's interest. This results in a geometric growth of funds. It snowballs and the bigger it gets, the bigger it gets.

Growth of money at compound interest progresses like a space rocket lifting off. Ever so slowly at first and then picking up speed until it finally reaches 17,000 MPH to escape earth's gravity. Young savers have the time advantage, but they often get impatient with the slow early growth and cash in the investment.

A little money and a lot of time can guarantee riches. In 1626 the Manhattan Indians sold their island to Dutch explorer

Peter Minuit for about $24. That value compounded at 6% to the year 2002 is 78.6 billion dollars.

If you are borrowing, ask for simple interest rather than compound. Simple interest is figured on the balance due without regard for time so there is no build up or stacking of money due.

Courses in business should be offered in middle and high school. Explain compound interest so the young person can know what the banks know, and explain the dangers of credit cards.

Give It Away and Then Sell It

In 1993, I acquired ½ acre on Black Creek. I took it in on trade. The man who bought the Palatka office owned it and he didn't want it anymore. The lot was located three miles west of Lake Asbury in Clay County, Florida. The lot had huge oaks and a high bank. You would never guess it could flood, but yet every few years it does flood. Only one or two feet of water covers the land and you can park on the hard road.

The trailer was 12' x 60', an older model. Mr. and Mrs. W were asleep when the water lapped in the front door and snuggled up to his nose. The trailer, contents, two cars and a tin shed 20' x 20' full of contents were all ruined. He got an insurance settlement with which he paid me $55,000 for Dad's office, but I gave him a $20,000 credit for the lot. His wet mess was now my wet mess.

My neighbor, Pionessa, was a contractor. For $2,300 he cleaned off the trailer and all other debris. He also cleared some of the land. One half acre left untended turns into jungle.

I priced the land at $29,500. I listed it with Watson Realty. I put it in multiple listing myself. I ran ads in the paper and mailed out data sheets. I dropped the price to $25,000.

Lightning struck a huge pine. I paid $1,000 for clearing that mess away. Kids opened the well spigot and the neighbor called me about the flood. I drove down and turned off the spigot. They also almost started a fire.

There were neighbors on both sides, so no serious dumping occurred. Taxes were $400 a year and mowing was $200 a year if you could get anyone to do it. I owned the lot five years. My total cost for this "free lot" was $5,000.

Newer homes are on pilings and the short street looks great. Check with someone about flooding. Realtors, neighbors or surveyors should know.

Property like this is price insensitive. You have to find a buyer who wants it. My efforts at selective price cutting were for naught.

In 1997, my daughter Stephanie needed money. I had been unable to sell the Black Creek lot, so I gave it to her.

I had never shown the land. There was any number of good sign calls that almost, but not quite, resulted in a contract. Two days after I gave her the deed, a man came by my office and paid $18,000. I got $4,000 and she got $14,000.

It took two more years for this money to be collected. At one point I had offered the lot for as little as $10,000.

In 1999 another buyer paid off Stephanie's mortgage, which came in handy for her wedding.

Mortgage Money

"That GI Bill was the best piece of legislation ever passed in the U.S. Congress, and made modern America. The suburbs, starting with Levittown and others, were paid for by GIs borrowing on their GI Bill at a very low interest rate. Thousands and thousands of small businesses were started in this country and are still there thanks to the loans from the GI Bill. It transformed our country." - Historian, Steven Ambrose.

The best lender is a local in-house lender. The money is local and decisions are made locally.

Next would be a big bank everyone has heard of and finally the broker. The broker charges a fee, but may be more convenient and respectful.

Your mortgage is likely to sell several times during its life. Lending is one of the most profitable businesses on earth.

The 30-year house mortgage does put a house within reach of almost everyone. It's expensive to create a mortgage so be careful about paying it off. If you sell or move, the extra money you've paid on the mortgage just went into a black hole. Only pay extra if you know you won't move and can pay off the whole thing.

Mortgage insurance protects the lender, not you. It pays off the balance if you default. It costs you money for this lender protection.

College finance courses teach hundreds of ways to borrow money, but the banks still have the tall buildings.

You can move a mortgage from one property to another with the lender's permission. This works best with the individual lender. He may want to preserve a higher than market interest loan, for example. This can be a cash conserver for the investor.

If the lender agrees, you can split or balloon a mortgage. The buyer of our fish camp was a terrible people person and he soon had no business. He asked for and received a lowered payment. Dad and Conrad got even more money by waiting, as the interest was not lowered.

Subordinating a mortgage means taking an inferior position to a new mortgage. You sell your land to a developer and hold the paper. The developer then proposes to build a shopping center and needs $1 million in funds. The bank will only lend if they have a first lien.

If you subordinate, you should increase the interest or get some other compensation for the increased risk; for if the project goes bad, you will have to pick up the obligation or lose your land.

It takes money to make money. Smart borrowing is a great wealth builder but, like fire, it can burn you.

Reverse Mortgage

FHA has underwritten a mortgage for senior citizen owners with no payments. If you are 62 or older, you can borrow on your homestead within the formula. I am 65 and can borrow $100,000 net on a value of $220,000. Debt accumulates and if it outstrips the value of the property at your death, the FHA eats it. They charge about 13% up front for this feature. Your heirs can inherit any remaining equity.

I have been in two classes now which demeaned the reverse mortgage as a poor person's salvation, but I think it is almost like free money. If you're sure you are going to stay in the home, it's good, but if you sell in a few years, you've paid a high price for a short term use of money, like usury (illegally high interest rate).

Use a mortgage person you trust and know to be competent and reliable, as these kinds of mortgages have imitators and are complicated.

By 2008, an ordinary citizen can use a reverse to buy a house. This seems like a powerful tool and a gift for the elderly and bad credit no problem.

Zoning and Growth

Zoning is government's power to regulate the use and density of your land. No money is paid, but rights are taken for the public good. Your property values increase because your neighbor can't put in a massage parlor.

People hate zoning changes even when they are good for them. Zoning violations should be reported by you, the citizen. Take photos and register a complaint if a guy opens a business in his home.

If you want to change your zoning, hire an attorney or Realtor experienced in zoning changes. You can do it yourself, but it's tricky. Your plan must be specific and you must make a good presentation in front of the board granting changes. Neighbors may hoot and yell and you have to stay calm.

Zoning is used to control growth. I favor infilling to reduce sprawl. Infilling is using land already in the city instead of on the edge or further out.

Traffic is lessened if close-in land is used. It's amazing how many acres are lying about vacant or with old vacant buildings.

Jacksonville is the city of the septic tank. This inhibits infilling. Good sewer lines must be available to encourage usage of close in land.

Enterprise zones are created to help beleaguered neighborhoods, both commercial and residential. Taxes should be abated in these areas, too.

The tear down is when a neighborhood of 2,000 sq. ft. homes has a prosperous citizen who tears down his home and builds a 5,000 sq. ft. mega three-story house. Neighbors complain because they lose their privacy and sun. Tear downs are a function of a prosperous economy and rising land values.

Finally, let's permit a garage we can live in. A mother-in-law building 20' x 24' could house a young couple struggling to make it and enter the economic mainstream. These could be built in conjunction with parent properties or on their own.

Deed Restrictions

These are private restrictions and may be found in the deed itself or more often recorded separately and cover the entire subdivision. They run with the land, unaffected by who owns the land, and are for a term of years, say 25 to 50 years.

They do the same thing as zoning, but the government will not enforce deed restrictions. The most infamous restrictions are those against racial minorities. "No racial minority of any kind may live in Magnolia Gardens unless they are servants and housed behind the main house." I presume that was the purpose of some garage apartments. Civil rights laws make restrictions of racial exclusivity null and void.

You must comply with zoning and deed restrictions. A professional person built an office on four-lane University Blvd. The building was up less than one year when it was torn down. They complied with zoning, but not restrictions which limited use to residential single family, even though the road was now commercial. Offended neighbors must bring suit to enforce deed restrictions. There is now a row of nice homes on the busy four-lane highway.

Deed restrictions can be created by will. They can apply to one property, as in a non-compete clause when a business is sold. I buy your restaurant, but you must not open another restaurant within two miles of the one I bought.

Old restrictions can be funny. All homes in Magnificent Acres must be at least $5,000 in cost. There shall be no outside privies and no homes made of cloth or metal. Kitchens shall be enclosed and no oil wells will be dug.

Bubbles

I have been through many recessions but the one we are in now is the 800 lb. gorilla.

The '74 recession was oil generated. The '81 recession was interest rate driven trying to quell the inflation caused by the '74 oil gouge. The '89 crash was the result of a few crooked savings and loan fellows riding a binge of deregulation. The dot com melt down of 2000 actually set real estate up for the next 6 years of hyper-inflation.

Today's problems are like the '29 crash in that poor over-sight and fraud touched it off. Corruption at Fannie Mae and the notion that everyone should own a house were at fault. Loans to unemployed people mixed with complicated mortgage derivatives exploded the financial markets. The securitization, or slicing and dicing piles of mortgages, makes it difficult to tell what the asset is worth and who has responsibility for it.

The 30 year mortgage made it possible for most people to own a home, but also set in motion inflationary pressure. As millions of new buyers flooded into the market, price rises were a given and written into text books as normal. Imagine my surprise to watch for the first time in my life values come down in 1989. It got little publicity then, but was a foretaste of today's housing deflation.

Lee Iacocca was a brilliant auto executive who gave us monthly payments. Buy a' 56 Ford for $56 a month for 3 years and there went waiting until you could afford it.

My parents paid rent of $65 a month for a 2 bedroom apartment until they bought their only house they lived in for $10,000 in 1963 which they paid off in 5 years.

All those people now upside down on their mortgage would have been better off renting.

We need to get back to working and giving more than we get to rebuild our shattered and lazy nation.

The short sale has kept the slump from being worse. Without shorts, foreclosures would have been more costly, more numerous and even worse for house values.

The collapse of the bubble cost about $7 trillion in United States housing value. By contrast, the World Trade Towers attack cost $15 billion.

Dad always said, "Things are going to come down." He didn't live to see it, but he was right, as to real estate prices.

Art

Dad didn't seem ambitious, but he saved money with a vengeance. He was handy and persistent. He liked everyone, but secretly disapproved of Democrats, Catholics and divorced people. He outlived all his seven siblings and inherited money from two of them.

He was weak on discipline, but had a strong will. It was decided for me that I was going to college. I got a degree but balked at being pushed into his fraternity. I ended up joining one that Mike Malaghan got me in.

The only thing Dad ever said about religion was that God helps those who help themselves!

Mother wouldn't marry any man unless he made at least $150 a month. Dad beat out another suitor who was "settin to her like a duck to a doe pile." With that being Dad's sole remark on romance, I had to develop my own sense of the romantic.

"What did you do in the war, Daddy?" He worked at a munitions plant at Las Vegas. He was too young for the first war and too old for the second.

Dad lived by the code of the Old West: "Never hit a man when he's down." Soon a drunk drove his jeep on top of a stump at the Florida fish camp. Dad went out to help, but the jeep wasn't cooperative, and the enraged drunk swung at Dad, grazing his ear. The force of the swing made the drunk fall down. Dad got mad and kicked him in the fanny.

He was patient to a fault. Kaplan from New York owned a prime piece of downtown Palatka. Dad serviced that listing for 20 years and no sale ever resulted, but Kaplan was kept up to speed on current events and value, all for free.

Mother died March 26, 1987. I wondered if Dad would go into a frenzy of deal making, since Mother was a harsh critic, but he did not. The only deal was selling Conrad's silver for $1,500 and giving the money to Stephanie and me.

Dad earned social security of $700 per month and interest income of $300 per month. He had no trouble getting along on $1,000. His house was paid for and expenses were low.

On April 19, 1988, Dad had heart surgery and was never the same. During the year we had without Mother prior to the surgery, he lectured me relentlessly about saving and thrift. As his recovery progressed, it was obvious his deal-making days were done, and I gradually took over his estate.

Dad lived on at Emmett Street, Palatka, Florida for six years.

We got out for errands. The first year I took him to the grocery store once a week, where he'd spend $12. After that, neighbors took him.

He sold his car for $1,500. I was elated, but the deal fell through when the car boiled over. Dr. Ahmad had told him not to drive, but Dad insisted we fix and re-fix his '77 Olds. I finally wrenched it away from him and sold it for $400.

His gun was stolen, and we filled out a police report. He eventually got it back and gave it to Hank, my ex father-in-law.

One day, when we took plastic flowers to Mother's grave, he introduced me to all the people he knew who were buried there.

The barber worked in his home across from the cemetery. He was also a preacher and, if you wanted, would "lay on hands" after cutting your hair. Dad outlived this barber, who was shot up in World War II.

We went to the bakery and various restaurants for lunch or snacks, and he chided me for leaving too big a tip. He said the waitresses would quit work if they got too big a tip. Dad was interesting and not that repetitive.

We bought a funeral package for $2,500, but he only wanted to pay $10 per month. Burial plots were already owned, for Mother and him. He assumed I would die moments after he did.

Doctor visits were a hoot. He'd rasp on about a "good BM" in the crowded waiting room, or say, "Bought an orange off a colored man today."

Dad, Stephanie, and I toured the Palatka nursing home. The halls were full of screaming Alzheimer patients. He wouldn't go there.

Finally the day came when he had no choice. He had fallen in the bathroom and was found the next day by the home care specialist prescribed by Dr. Ahmad. After a hospital stay, he was moved to Eagle Crest nursing home in Jacksonville.

April 19, 1994 Dad was "interred" and lived there for the next four years. He was approved for Medicaid, so all his medical was paid by taxpayers. The heart surgery, hip surgery, and nursing care expenses were about $300,000. They got his social security.

Dad still "worked." He'd stand or sit by the door, and open it for people. One day I dropped in about lunchtime, and he was seated at a 10-person table. He said, "These are the presidents," waving his arms at the other residents.

Once in Jacksonville, the problems were not over. Medical needs required me to take or accompany him to the dentist, heart doctor, blood man and so on. Social services tried to help, but the work it caused me compounded. One time I took him to Gainesville to a cancer specialist.

A woman heart doctor asked Dad, "How'd you break your hip?" Dad enthused, "I fell off a horse." She asked him if he wanted a pacemaker. Dad's libido leaped to the forefront and he smiled, "Anything you want is OK with me."

He brightened at the sight of me or Stephanie. He called me fat to the end. He'd whisper and rasp. I'd lean in, thinking he might tell me about some missing brother or sister, but it didn't happen.

He couldn't understand me, but could understand my answers to his questions. I became Conrad.

He never said he loved me in his life, but he did say I was a good son. He said, "I'll be glad when this war is over."

I allowed a feeding tube, but he continued to lose weight and died September 22, 1998 at 97 years old.

I see him in dreams, those gifts from God.

Relax

At last, a real estate book written by someone who is not successful.

Coming soon on this site: Ordinary condominiums

Florida would be nothing without drainage ditches, air-conditioning and bug spray.

Don't use a property management office with a broken window.

Expense of decor has little to do with value added.

Pay your appraiser's bill because he could be elected tax assessor.

He broke up with his girl friend, so he bought the house next door.

Don't use a ceiling fan in a barbershop

'The trouble with jobs is you have to show up and wear socks.

Don't put a boat ramp next to a bar.

Realtors look on a mortgage interest deduction like a father with a virgin daughter.

Don't build a casket factory next to a hospital.

If your husband buys a restaurant, you will be a waitress!

Appraisers should be brave, but not foolish.

Be first in a small town. Gene Buchanan got the first State Farm Agency in Palatka and had it all to himself for 25 years.

Don't trust a dog to watch your food.

The employer said, "I will pay you what you are worth." The interviewee said, "I will not accept it." Don't take a beer to your job interview.

How can you spot a rich real estate developer in a crowd? His wife and daughter are the same age.

The young appraiser is met at the house by a saleswoman. He looks inside and says, "Yuck! What bad taste they've got!" The abashed woman says, "This is my house."

A Realtor was showing a house when a fleeing criminal ran across the front yard. Following him was a police officer, who tackled the felon and cuffed him. The amazed buyer's jaw dropped. The Realtor quickly regained his composure, saying, "High profile police work."

Accident Attorney: "Your broken butt is my good luck."

Sell your lake land while the lake has water in it.

When accountants design clothes, pockets are left off.

Traffic planners should not make a one-way street a dead end.

Encyclopedias for sale, wife knows everything.

Be lucky. Work hard and strike oil. The harder you work the luckier you get.

Nothing has value like a lost lotto ticket. The passing of time cures all problems. Don't argue over what to do with lotto winnings.

You can go wrong taking a profit, if you could have gotten a bigger profit. The first half of goal is go. Today's rip-off is tomorrow's good deal.

Appraising, it's important to get the first digit right. Is it $700,000 or $800,000?

Part of something is better than all of nothing.

A saying of old is: "Harry drowned in a stream of 6" average depth."

Dad had a record from the Board of Realtors by Earl Nightingale. It said, "We become what we think about." It compared our mind to a garden that grew whatever was planted there.

In the movie Bruce Almighty "God" says to Bruce, "If you want a miracle, be a miracle."

It's not how long you have to work, but how long you are able to work that's important.

If you get unexpected money, are you happy to get it or unhappy it wasn't more?

Poverty is a great teacher. Need breeds creativity. Being rich means waste and indolence is encouraged.

You are only as strong as the table you dance on (thanks Josie).

Don't invest in a dog bakery. If a dog bakery owner has a dog, it will be fat.

Jerry bought 10 talking/singing catfish as an investment.

Whoever has the best garbage can on the street will have it stolen.

The well known term "going downhill" is literal in housing. The good homes are high up and lesser ones lower in elevation.

Busyholicness is the urge to make a deal even if it is a bad deal.

One of the best things you can do for yourself and your kids is to have a life of your own.

Everyone dies famous in a small town (country song).

If a house has a wrecker parked there, junk cars will soon follow.

The devil is said to have offices in Purgatory, Hell, and Los Angeles.

Don't send a Snoopy sympathy card. Don't insult your bodyguard.

Don't buy a house on a street with speed bumps.

A woman called wanting a "true" appraisal. Is slanting of appraisals that big a problem?

Walking on water is easy if you know where the stones are.

One good investment is worth a lifetime of toil, but don't quit your job.

The wrong side of the tracks is where the brothels were.

Wells Fargo thumped ATM's in 1988 as a brash and stupid idea.

The old investor now has more doctors than condominiums.

Realtors should be careful about locating in a town with no new construction visible.

About The Author

Jeff Cooper was born in Las Vegas, Nevada in 1943. His parents, Art and Ione Cooper, left Pittsburgh in 1950 to buy a fish camp, Magnolia Bluff, south of Palatka, Florida.

Jeff graduated from Palatka High School, an honor student. He received a bachelor's degree from the University of Florida in 1965 in real estate. From 1966 to 1972 he served in the Army Reserve as an enlisted man.

His first job was with Howze & Associates as a real estate tax appraiser. From 1968 to 1970, he worked for John Rogers and Earl Miller in Jacksonville, Florida as a fee appraiser.

Jeff opened his own office in 1970, called Jeff Cooper Company, not Inc. on the Arlington Expressway. He taught real estate classes for the junior college. In 1973, he merged with Art Cooper, forming Jeff Cooper Company, Inc. The Palatka office closed upon Art's retirement in 1988.

Jeff currently resides in Jacksonville with his wife Martha. Jeff's daughters are Stephanie, Kim, Karen, and Kelli.

1970 -joined Jacksonville Board of Realtors.

1975 -approved for VA appraisal panel.

1990-became certified residential appraiser (number RD680) per Florida law.

Appraisal clients served include: Fannie Mae, Freddie Mac, City of Jacksonville, City of Palatka, Clay Electric, Duval County School Board, FDIC, Georgia Pacific, BellSouth, Chevron, Urban Renewal Authority, Gulf Oil, Phillips Petroleum, 7-Eleven, State Farm Insurance, SBA, Wells Fargo, Episcopal Diocese, Seaboard Railroad, Ford Motor Company, FHA, VA (Veterans Administration), and the State of Florida.

Contact:

Jeff Cooper, 819 Acapulco Road, Jacksonville, Fl 32216, phone 904-724-6000, fax 904-725-5530, res. 904-725-4260, email: Jcconrad@bellsouth.net

This book can be bought from Amazon.com, Barnes & Noble, or any online outlet. It is also an "E" book.